WITHDRAWN

Wake Tech. Libraries
9101 Fayetteville Road
Raleigh, North Carolina 27603-5696

Building the Nation

1791–1832

Titles in the Series

From Colonies to a Country 1635–1790

Building the Nation 1791–1832

A Country Divided 1833–1868

Entering the Industrial Age 1869–1933

A World Power 1934 to the Present

DEBATABLE ISSUES IN U.S. HISTORY

VOLUME TWO

Building the Nation

1791–1832

GREENWOOD PRESS
Westport, Connecticut · London

Library of Congress Cataloging-in-Publication Data

Debatable issues in U.S. history / by Creative Media Applications.
      p. cm.—(Middle school reference)
   Includes bibliographical references and index.
ISBN 0–313–32910–9 (set : alk. paper)—ISBN 0–313–32911–7 (v. 1 : alk. paper)—
ISBN 0–313–32912–5 (v. 2 : alk. paper)—ISBN 0–313–32913–3 (v. 3 : alk. paper)—
ISBN 0–313–32914–1 (v. 4 : alk. paper)—ISBN 0–313–32915–X (v. 5 : alk. paper)
   1. United States—History—Miscellanea—Juvenile literature.
2. United States—Politics and government—Miscellanea—Juvenile literature.
3. United States—Social conditions—Miscellanea—Juvenile literature.
4. Critical thinking—Study and teaching (Middle school)—United States.
[1. United States—History. 2. United States—Politics and
government.] I. Creative Media Applications. II. Series.
E178.3.D35   2004
973—dc22   2003056802

British Library Cataloguing in Publication Data is available.

Copyright © 2004 by Greenwood Publishing Group, Inc.

All rights reserved. No portion of this book may be reproduced, by any process or technique, without the express written consent of the publisher.

Library of Congress Catalog Card Number: 2003056802
ISBN: 0–313–32910–9 (set)
           0–313–32911–7 (vol. 1)
           0–313–32912–5 (vol. 2)
           0–313–32913–3 (vol. 3)
           0–313–32914–1 (vol. 4)
           0–313–32925–X(vol. 5)

First published in 2004

Greenwood Press, 88 Post Road West, Westport, CT 06881
An imprint of Greenwood Publishing Group, Inc.
www.greenwood.com

Printed in the United States of America

The paper used in this book complies with the Permanent Paper Standard issued by the National Information Standards Organization (Z39.48–1984).

10 9 8 7 6 5 4 3 2 1

A Creative Media Applications, Inc. Production
Writer: Michael Burgan
Design and Production: Fabia Wargin Design
Editor: Matt Levine
Copyeditor: Laurie Lieb
Proofreader: Betty Pessagno
Indexer: Nara Wood
Associated Press Photo Researcher: Yvette Reyes
Consultant: Mel Urofsky, Professor Emeritus of History at Virginia Commonwealth University

Photo credits:
AP/Wide World Photographs *pages* 5, 31, 32, 33, 40, 41, 46, 59, 105, 120
© CORBIS *page* 6
© PictureHistory *pages* 8, 63, 67, 73, 77, 80, 85, 88, 95, 98, 107, 123
© Hulton Archives/Getty Images *pages* 11, 17, 19, 21, 27, 49, 51, 53, 71, 78, 92, 102, 110, 117, 118, 125
© Bettmann/CORBIS *pages* 24, 61, 113, 126
© North Wind Picture Archives *page* 43

Contents

Introduction		7
CHAPTER ONE:	Jay's Treaty	11
CHAPTER TWO:	The Alien and Sedition Acts	21
CHAPTER THREE:	The Election of 1800	31
CHAPTER FOUR:	The Louisiana Purchase	41
CHAPTER FIVE:	The Burr Conspiracy	51
CHAPTER SIX:	The Embargo of 1808	63
CHAPTER SEVEN:	The War of 1812	73
CHAPTER EIGHT:	The Missouri Compromise	85
CHAPTER NINE:	Early Industry	95
CHAPTER TEN:	The Election of 1824	105
CHAPTER ELEVEN:	The Rise of the Abolitionist Movement	113
CHAPTER TWELVE:	The Nullification Crisis	123
Glossary		133
Bibliography		134
Cumulative Index		135

Open debate among its citizens is one of the most important characteristics of a democratic nation like the United States. This 1851 engraving shows a public debate being held in Boston on the issue of slavery. Speaking is Wendell Phillips, a leading Boston abolitionist (a person who was working to end slavery).

Introduction

When people come together in a community, they face important decisions about how to run their affairs. Since everyone does not think alike, have the same feelings, or share the same interests, disagreements often arise over key issues.

In a democratic society such as the United States, public debate helps leaders decide what action to take on the most important issues. The debates might start in Congress or another branch of the government. They are often carried on in the media, and they continue in homes, in offices, and wherever concerned citizens gather.

How much power should the national government have?

The five volumes of *Debatable Issues in U.S. History* look at some of the most important issues that have sparked political and social debates, from colonial times to the present day. Some of the issues have been local, such as the dispute between Roger Williams and the Puritan leaders of Massachusetts. Williams struggled to introduce the idea of religious freedom in a community that wanted just one kind of religious worship. Other issues—segregation, for example—had special significance for a large group of people. African Americans, who had once been forced to live in slavery, had to endure lingering prejudice even when they received their freedom during and after the Civil War (1861–1865). Some of the most important issues have touched all Americans, as the country's leaders considered whether to go to war in times of international crisis. The 2003 war in Iraq is just the latest example of that debate.

Throughout American history, certain types of issues have appeared over and over. The details may change, but Americans continue to argue over such things as: How much power should the national government have? How does society balance personal freedom with the need to protect the common good? Which political party has the best vision for strengthening the country? Who should America choose as its friends and its enemies around the world?

> How does society balance personal freedom with the need to protect the common good?

Historians have debated the importance of certain events for hundreds of years. New facts emerge, or interpretations change as the world changes. From the historians' view, almost any issue is debatable. This series, however, focuses on the events and issues that Americans debated as they occurred. Today, few people would question whether the American colonies should have declared their independence from Great Britain; it seems almost impossible to imagine anything else happening. However, to the Americans of the day, the issue was not so clear-cut. Colonial leaders strongly disagreed on what action to take in the months before Thomas Jefferson wrote the Declaration of Independence.

Debate over important issues has been a vital component of life in the United States since the very beginning. In the first decade of the 1800s, for instance, there was debate about the Embargo Act, a group of laws that affected trade with European countries. This political cartoon from the time pokes fun at the debaters.

At times in the past, debate over key issues might have been limited. From the seventeenth century through most of the nineteenth century, transportation and communication were primitive compared with today. Still, through letters, sermons, newspapers, and government documents, opposing ideas were shared and debated. The lack of electronic communication did not weaken the passion with which people held their beliefs and their desire to shape public issues.

Today, the Internet and other forms of digital communication let millions of people debate crucial issues that face the United States. Better technology, however, does not make it easier for people to settle these issues. As *Debatable Issues in U.S. History* shows, strong emotions often fuel the discussions over the issues. At times, those emotions spill out in violence. On issues that matter most, people are often unwilling to give in, modify their views, or admit that they are wrong. Those attitudes can lead to debates that last for generations. Abortion was a heated issue in 1973, when the U.S. Supreme Court ruled that a woman could legally have an abortion if she chose. Abortion remains a divisive issue today, and there is not much chance that the debate will end.

> Who should America choose as its friends and its enemies around the world?

Debates and disagreements can make it hard for governments to function smoothly. Still, debate allows Americans to explore all sides of an issue. Debate can also lead to new and better ideas that no one had considered before. U.S. Supreme Court Justice William Brennan once noted that Americans have "a profound national commitment to the principle that debate on public issues should be uninhibited, robust, and wide open." That commitment first took shape in colonial America, and it continues today.

A Note to the Reader

The quotations in Debatable Issues in U.S. History *are taken from primary sources, the writings and speeches of the people debating the important issues of their time. Some of the words, phrases, and images in these sources may be offensive by today's standards, but they are an authentic example of our past history. Also, some of the quotes have been slightly changed to reflect the modern spelling of the original words or to make the meaning of the quotes clearer. All metric conversions in this book are approximate.*

CHAPTER ONE

Jay's Treaty

WHAT
The United States and Great Britain sign a treaty
settling several issues between them.

ISSUE
Relations with Great Britain and France
and their effect on U.S. politics

WHERE
Treaty signed in London, England

WHEN
1794–1795

U.S. political parties began taking shape soon after George Washington became the first president under the new Constitution. By the early 1790s, his cabinet began to split along distinct lines. Secretary of the Treasury Alexander Hamilton led a faction that promoted the strongest possible national government. Hamilton also backed foreign trade—especially with Great Britain—and building new industries. Secretary of State Thomas Jefferson, meanwhile, tended to fear the power of a strong national government. He supported the country's farming interests, and he favored keeping good relations with France. Other people who shared these beliefs formed a second political faction. After stepping down as secretary of state at the end of 1793, Jefferson remained a leader of this faction.

Americans who supported Hamilton and his policies formed what became the Federalist Party. Jefferson and his supporters—who included James Madison, the main author of the Constitution—were known as Democratic-Republicans. One major difference between the two parties was the way that their members felt about Great Britain. The Federalists saw a natural connection between Americans and the British. They shared a language, similar political beliefs, and a common history. Hamilton also believed that the U.S. economy would grow if Americans made the British their major trading partner. The Democratic-Republicans, however, believed that Great Britain could not be trusted. They thought that it would use its economic power to hurt U.S. interests.

Different opinions about France also divided the Federalists and Democratic-Republicans. Federalists believed that the French Revolution (1789–1799) threatened order across Europe and feared that the radical actions taking place in France could spread to the United States. Democratic-Republicans, however, generally welcomed the French Revolution. Just as the Americans had done in

Fast Fact

The Democratic-Republicans of the late eighteenth century are sometimes called Jeffersonian Republicans to distinguish them from today's Republican Party.

1776, the French had thrown off royal rule and established a republican government. Early in 1793, Jefferson claimed that "universal feasts, and rejoicings" broke out across America to celebrate the French Revolution.

> *Fast Fact*
>
> In 1791, Great Britain bought half of the goods that Americans sent overseas, and Americans bought 90 percent of their foreign goods from the British.

Wartime Troubles

The French Revolution took a dramatic turn in 1793. That spring, Americans learned that the French had killed their former king, Louis XVI, and declared war on England and Spain. These actions confirmed the Federalists' beliefs that the French revolutionaries were dangerous. Hamilton argued that the United States should end a treaty of friendship that it had signed with France in 1778. Most Democratic-Republicans, however, continued to support the French Revolution, and Jefferson said that the United States should still honor the 1778 treaty. In the end, President Washington did honor the treaty, but he said that the United States would remain neutral in the war between France and Great Britain.

Soon, the French began hiring private American ships to capture British merchant ships, which angered the British. Then the British began capturing American ships carrying food to the French West Indies, islands in the Caribbean Sea. The British also encouraged Native Americans in the western United States to step up an ongoing war with American troops.

These actions came on top of some long-standing problems between Great Britain and its former colonies. At the end of the American Revolution (1775–1783), the British agreed to vacate forts along the Great Lakes that were in U.S. territory, but in 1794, British troops were still there. The British also refused to pay for slaves that they had freed or taken with them during and after the war. On the other side, the British had their own complaint against the Americans. State governments had refused to help the British collect debts that were owed to them from before the Revolution.

Responding to the new problems with Great Britain, Congress voted to end trade with that country for several months. Hamilton feared that this action, called an embargo, could lead to war. To try to improve U.S.-British relations, Washington named John Jay as a special envoy, or diplomat, to Great Britain.

Jay's job was to prevent a war and address some of the issues between the two countries. Jay was not happy with the assignment. Federalists and Democratic-Republicans had such strong, opposing feelings about Great Britain that neither side would be completely happy with any treaty. The mission, he feared, would end his political career. Still, Jay said that "the good of my country I believe demands the sacrifice, and I am ready to make it."

Jay's Treaty

Jay arrived in London, England, in June 1794. He had two major instructions about what he could and could not do. He could not make any agreements that harmed U.S. relations with France, as spelled out in the 1778 treaty, and he could not sign any treaty on trade that did not allow U.S. ships to bring goods to British islands in the West Indies.

Although it had a much stronger military than the United States, Great Britain did not want to use its ships and troops to fight the Americans. Defeating the French would require as much firepower as possible. The British also did not want to disrupt their important trade with the United States. Still, the British were not going to give in to all of the U.S. demands. As the wealthier country, Great Britain had the upper hand.

In the final treaty, the British agreed to pull their troops out of the Northwest. However, they did not

> *Fast Fact*
> In the United States, a treaty must be ratified by two-thirds of all U.S. senators. The actual Senate vote approving Jay's Treaty was twenty to ten—exactly two-thirds.

agree to pay for the slaves taken during the war, and they kept the right to seize some American goods bound for France or French goods on U.S. ships. The Americans also did not get the trading rights that they wanted. The two sides agreed to settle some issues, such as pre-Revolution debts, in the future.

The details of Jay's Treaty reached U.S. officials in March 1795. Hamilton backed it, believing that it would prevent war and that it was the best treaty the United States could get at the time. Democratic-Republicans, however, strongly attacked the treaty, saying that it favored the British. After a long debate, the Senate ratified, or approved, the treaty by the slimmest possible margin.

THE IMPRESSMENT ISSUE

One disagreement between the United States and Great Britain came over impressment. In this practice, British naval ships stopped U.S. merchant ships to search for British citizens who had deserted British ships. In some cases, U.S. citizens were wrongly accused of being British deserters, taken from their ships, and forced to serve on British ships. Some Democratic-Republicans wanted Jay to address this problem, but the issue was not mentioned in the final treaty. The impressments continued, and they later played a role in sparking a war between the United States and Great Britain—the War of 1812 (1812–1815).

The Democratic-Republicans Attack the Treaty

American citizens did not learn about the details of the treaty until after the Senate vote. At that time, Washington had still not officially signed the treaty. Before he did, Democratic-Republican protests broke out in many cities. The Democratic-Republicans did not want any agreement that seemed to help Great Britain in any way while it was at war with France.

Jay's Treaty also seemed to weaken U.S. support for France, while the 1778 treaty with France said that the two nations would support each other. Robert Livingston of New York said that Jay's Treaty "sacrifices our friends to our enemies." In the treaty, the United States largely accepted the British definition of neutral shipping rights. That definition favored the British over the French. Livingston and others also complained that the treaty did not address impressment.

Democratic-Republicans in general also opposed anything supported by Hamilton. To them, Hamilton and other leading Federalists were monarchists—people who favored a king to lead the government or used the same kind of tactics that a king might use. The public only learned about the treaty's details after a Democratic-Republican senator gave them to a reporter. Until then, the U.S. Senate had been discussing the treaty in secret. One Democratic-Republican senator accused the Federalists of "practicing all the secrecy of monarchy, so opposite to open and republican principles."

> *Fast Fact*
> Because of Democratic-Republican protests, the final version of Jay's Treaty did not include the section limiting trade with the British West Indies.

Perhaps the strongest complaint arose over the issues of U.S. trade in the British West Indies. The restriction hurt Southern farmers who grew cotton and Northern shippers who carried it. The restriction also attacked the notion of free trade, which many Americans supported. James Madison wrote, "If we hold at present the rank of a free people…we have the self-evident right, to regulate our trade according to our own will." Madison said that the U.S. government should be placing limits on British trade with America to punish the British for carrying out policies that hurt U.S. interests.

Famous Figures

JOHN JAY
(1745–1829)

A wealthy New York lawyer, John Jay was one of the last major political figures of the American Revolution to support independence. Once he joined the cause, he held several important positions in the first U.S. governments. In 1779, he served as president of the Continental Congress, and four years later, he helped draft the treaty that ended the Revolution. A leading Federalist, Jay supported Hamilton's efforts to build a strong national government. Washington named him as the first chief justice of the U.S. Supreme Court. After Jay's mission to Great Britain in 1794, he left national politics and served as governor of New York for six years.

TARGETING JAY

Many Democratic-Republicans directed their anger over Jay's Treaty and Federalist policies at John Jay himself. In some cities, protesters made dummies representing Jay and hung them from trees and burned them. Some historians suggest that Jay's unpopularity after the treaty cost him the chance of ever running for president, as he had wanted to do.

In Their Own Words

Here is part of an article that James Madison wrote attacking Jay's Treaty.

Indeed, the treaty from one end to the other must be regarded as a demonstration that the [Federalist Party] is a British party systematically aiming at an exclusive connection with the British government and ready to sacrifice to that object...the dearest interests of our commerce...[and] the most sacred dictates of our national honor.

The Federalists Defend the Treaty

Although Hamilton left Washington's cabinet at the start of 1795, he still advised the president on many issues. He led the Federalist effort to approve and defend Jay's Treaty. In one article, he noted that the Democratic-Republicans had come out against the treaty even before they knew its details. They were not arguing against specific points; they simply did not want any treaty with Great Britain. Hamilton thought that the treaty's leading opponents were "enemies of the national government." Anyone with an open mind, Hamilton wrote, would see that "the treaty adjusts, in a reasonable manner, the points in controversy between the United States and Great Britain."

Hamilton pointed out that under the new treaty, the British would finally leave their forts—which the Americans could then use in their war against Native Americans. Hamilton also noted that the United States had not done everything that it was supposed to do under the 1783 Treaty of Paris, which had ended the American Revolution. He argued that the states' efforts to stop the repayment of debts owed to the British was an attack on one of the most important rights—the right to own and keep private property.

President George Washington's first cabinet, from left to right: Secretary of War Henry Knox, Secretary of State Thomas Jefferson, Attorney General Edmund Randolph (with back turned), Secretary of the Treasury Alexander Hamilton, and Washington himself. Jefferson and Hamilton would soon represent rival political parties whose differences were at the center of the debate over Jay's Treaty.

One of Hamilton's main arguments was that Jay's Treaty preserved peace between the United States and Great Britain. The United States was not prepared to fight a war, despite its recent effort to build a navy and spend more on defense. "We ought to see," he wrote, "that this is not a time for trying our strength." Even if the treaty had problems, avoiding a war should be the country's main concern at the time.

In the end, Hamilton's arguments carried more weight in Congress and with Washington. Jefferson noted that the Democratic-Republicans had "only middling performances to oppose him." Until his death in 1804, Hamilton continued to influence Federalist policies, which included pursuing the best possible relations with Great Britain and opposing the French.

In Their Own Words

Here is part of a report Hamilton wrote to George Washington on Jay's Treaty.

The truly most important side of this treaty is that it closes... upon the whole...the controverted points between the two countries...and...[preserves] ourselves in a state of peace for a considerable time to come....With peace, the force of circumstances will enable us to make our way sufficiently fast in trade. War at this time would give a serious wound to our growth and prosperity.

THE BATTLE GOES ON

The Democratic-Republican protests continued even after Washington signed the treaty in August 1795. In the spring of 1796, the U.S. House of Representatives debated whether to spend the money needed to carry out the treaty. Democratic-Republicans tried to block the funding and lost on a close vote.

CHAPTER TWO

The Alien and Sedition Acts

WHAT
Congress passes laws to restrict the activities of certain immigrants and prevent written and spoken attacks on the U.S. government.

ISSUES
Direction of foreign and domestic policies; fear of foreign influence in the United States; protection of personal liberties

WHERE
Nationwide

WHEN
1798

During the 1790s, Americans watched events in Europe with growing concern. In 1789, the French had started a revolution to end the power of their king and create a republican form of government—the kind used in the United States. By 1793, the revolution had turned increasingly bloody, and the French executed their last king, Louis XVI. That same year, France declared war on Great Britain.

As the war went on, Americans took sides for and against Great Britain and France. On one side were the Federalists. Led by Alexander Hamilton, they supported Great Britain. In domestic politics, they favored a strong national government and promoted commerce. The first two U.S. presidents, George Washington and John Adams, were Federalists. Opposing them were the Democratic-Republicans. Thomas Jefferson was considered their leader, and they generally supported the French Revolution (1789–1799) and France's war against the British. Democratic-Republicans believed that the British posed a greater threat to U.S. interests than the French did. Democratic-Republicans tended to distrust the power of the central government under Federalist rule.

In 1793, Washington declared that the United States would remain neutral in the European war. The next year, however, the United States signed Jay's Treaty with Great Britain. In the treaty, the United States accepted British actions limiting its trade with France. At first, the French responded by trying to influence U.S. politics. French representatives in the United States spoke out against the treaty and openly supported Jefferson in the 1796 presidential election against John Adams. (Jefferson lost but was named vice president.)

Next, the French turned to military action. Their naval ships began capturing U.S. merchant ships carrying goods in the Caribbean Sea. By the summer of 1797, the French had seized

> *Fast Fact*
> In the first three presidential elections, the candidate who finished second was named vice president. This system changed in 1804, when voters started electing the president and vice president separately.

more than 300 U.S. ships. President Adams wrote that he hoped to end the difficulties with France through diplomacy, "provided that no...stain upon honor, is exacted."

The XYZ Affair and Calls for War

In October 1797, three U.S. representatives arrived in France to meet with Talleyrand (born Charles Maurice de Talleyrand-Périgord), the French foreign minister. Through several agents, Talleyrand told the Americans that they would have to agree to loan money to France before he would deal with them. The foreign minister also wanted the U.S. diplomats to give money to him personally. The Americans refused, and the talks ended.

In March 1798, Adams learned about the failed talks and Talleyrand's demand for bribes. He called on Congress to prepare for a possible war with France. Jefferson and other Democratic-Republicans demanded to know why Adams was preparing for war. The president released messages from the U.S. diplomats describing the attempted bribes and bad treatment that they had received. Adams did not release the names of Talleyrand's agents; they were only referred to as X, Y, and Z.

Many Americans reacted angrily when they heard the details of the "XYZ affair." Most supported Adams and his policies, which included ending all previous treaties with France. The country was moving toward an undeclared war, with Congress calling for new naval ships and army divisions. The government also gave armed American merchant ships the right to attack French ships that tried to search them.

Democratic-Republicans, however, did not join in praising Adams and calling for war. Democratic-Republican newspapers, such as the *Aurora* of Philadelphia, Pennsylvania, continued to speak out against the Federalists and for the French. In the meantime, the Federalists were preparing to take steps against the French in the United States and any Americans who supported them.

This political cartoon is about the XYZ affair of 1797. The Americans on the left are resisting the threats made by the five-headed "Paris Monster," who is demanding money from them. Differences of opinion about the XYZ affair underscored the dispute between the Federalist and the Democratic-Republican political parties in the United States.

The Alien and Sedition Acts

Starting in June 1798, Congress, under Federalist control, began passing a series of laws known as the Alien and Sedition Acts. The first, the Naturalization Act, said that aliens—people born in foreign countries who settled in the United States—had to wait fourteen years before they could be naturalized, or become U.S. citizens. Before this law, the waiting period was five years. The Federalists wanted to make it harder for immigrants to become citizens. Once immigrants were naturalized, they won the right to vote, and many recent immigrants supported the Democratic-Republicans.

The next law, the Alien Friends Act, gave the president the power to force aliens out of the country during war or peacetime, if the president thought that they threatened U.S. security. The law had a two-year limit. The Alien Enemies Act applied only during wartime. Any alien males from a country at war with the

United States automatically became enemies. They could be arrested and forced out of the country. This law had no time limit.

The last law led to the most anger between Democratic-Republicans and Federalists. The Sedition Act was designed to prevent public attacks on the government, whether spoken or written. The law addressed the legal concept of seditious libel—words criticizing government officials and their actions that might lead to social unrest. People could also be punished if their words were thought to hurt the government's reputation or weaken public support for it. The Sedition Act set definite fines and prison terms for anyone found guilty of seditious libel. The new law had a time limit of two years. President Adams had not asked Congress to pass the Sedition Act, but he clearly supported its goal of clamping down on anti-Federalist statements.

> *Fast Fact*
> The Federalists wrote the Sedition Act so that it expired on March 3, 1801—the last day of John Adams's term as president. This guaranteed that the law stayed in effect through the presidential campaign of 1800.

The Sedition Act led to the most debate and had the greatest impact on American citizens. Although the law said that truth was a defense against the charge of seditious libel, some judges and juries ignored this. They convicted a few people even though what they had said or written was true or was an opinion that would be hard to prove either true or false.

The Democratic-Republicans Attack the Acts

In Congress and the press, Democratic-Republicans criticized the Alien and Sedition Acts. They saw that most of the laws were aimed at weakening their political influence and attacking their supporters across the country. Albert Gallatin, a Democratic-Republican representative from Pennsylvania, led many of the Democratic-Republican efforts to oppose or weaken the four laws.

> **Fast Fact**
>
> The Naturalization Act was directed mainly at the Irish. Ireland was rebelling against British rule, and Irish immigrants in America tended to be anti-British and pro-French.

When the Naturalization Act was debated, the Democratic-Republicans saw a Federalist attack on the patriotism of foreign-born Americans. Gallatin and the Democratic-Republicans were able to defeat a Federalist effort to make the law apply to aliens already in the country, not just new arrivals, but they could not reduce the time limit, as they had hoped, or prevent its approval.

Against the other two alien laws, the Democratic-Republicans had a variety of complaints. They claimed that keeping out aliens, or forcing them out once they arrived, was a power that belonged to the states, not the national government. In a general way, the Democratic-Republicans claimed that the alien laws gave the national government too much power and threatened liberty in the United States. In particular, Edward Livingston of New York said that the Alien Enemies Act was unconstitutional. "By [the alien law]," he said, "the president alone is empowered to make the law, to fix in his mind what act, what words…shall constitute the crime contemplated by the bill." Under the Constitution, Livingston said, the president did not have that power.

The Democratic-Republicans reacted most strongly to the Sedition Act. Their attacks helped soften the language of the law. As the Federalists first wrote it, the Sedition Act would have punished true, as well as false, words. The proposed law also specifically said that supporting France in any way was treason. These two ideas were not in the final bill.

The Democratic-Republicans once again turned to the Constitution to argue against the Sedition Act. The law clearly went against the First Amendment, which guaranteed freedom of speech and of the press. Limiting what people could say or write, the Democratic-Republicans argued, weakened republican government. "The heart and life of free government," said one representative, "is a free press; take this away, and you take away its main support."

In two states, Kentucky and Virginia, lawmakers did more than speak out against the Sedition Act. They claimed that they and other states had a right to reject the law completely, since it was not constitutional. In Virginia, James Madison wrote a series of resolutions, or public statements, that argued this point. Thomas Jefferson wrote a similar set of resolutions for Kentucky. The Kentucky and Virginia Resolutions later served as models for other states that claimed that they did not have to follow unconstitutional laws.

Famous Figures
ALBERT GALLATIN
(1761–1849)

Born in Switzerland, Albert Gallatin settled in Pennsylvania in 1780. His foreign birth, as well as his Democratic-Republican ideas, stirred Federalist suspicion of his political goals. Gallatin served in the Pennsylvania legislature before holding seats in both the U.S. Senate and House of Representatives. From 1801 to 1814, Gallatin was secretary of the treasury under Presidents Thomas Jefferson and James Madison. Later, he served as a U.S. diplomat.

In Their Own Words

Here is part of Albert Gallatin's speech in the House of Representatives against the Sedition Act.

If you put the press under any restraint in respect to the measures of members of government; if you thus deprive the people of the means of obtaining information of their conduct, you in fact render their right of electing [worthless]; and this bill must be considered only as a weapon used by a party now in power in order to [continue] their authority and preserve their present places.

The Federalists Argue for the Acts

Fast Fact

States had their own laws on citizenship, and immigrants could become citizens of a state before applying for U.S. citizenship. In some states, immigrants had to wait only one or two years to become citizens.

The Federalists claimed that the Alien and Sedition Acts were designed to end a foreign threat and protect the government. With the Naturalization Act, the Federalists hoped to limit the role of the foreign-born in U.S. politics. Many Federalists believed that new immigrants caused most of the country's problems. Forced to wait fourteen years to become citizens, many immigrants might not bother to do so. The most extreme Federalists wanted to deny immigrants any chance to become citizens, but their views were rejected.

The concern about immigrants also led to the Alien Enemies and Alien Friends Acts. The enemies act focused specifically on the supposed threat from French immigrants as the United States and France moved close to war. Some Federalists claimed that France was sending spies to America to weaken the country from within. One Federalist paper said there were enough spies to "burn all our cities and cut the throats of all the inhabitants."

The Alien Enemies Act was supposed to protect the country during this time of crisis with France. Many Federalists, however, also believed that the country could be threatened by people from other countries. That thinking led to the Alien Friends Act. "The times are full of danger," Harrison Gray Otis of Massachusetts said, "and it would be the height of madness not to take every precaution in our power." Otis believed that the French might send citizens from other countries to America to carry out attacks on its government and people.

The Federalists used the possibility of French attacks as one reason for passing the Sedition Act. The Federalists claimed that every government had the right to protect itself from seditious libel. The First Amendment, they said, did not weaken that right. In a time of crisis, the Federalists believed, the press and politicians should not criticize the government, since the people might lose faith in it. Under the Constitution, Congress had the right to pass laws that let it carry out its duties. Punishing seditious libel was the only way to make sure that the government operated smoothly.

In Their Own Words

Here is part of a speech by Connecticut congressman John Allen defending the Sedition Act.

The president of the United States is here called "a person without patriotism, without philosophy, and a mock monarch."... Because the Constitution guarantees the right of expressing our opinions and the freedom of the press, am I at liberty to falsely call you a thief, a murderer, an atheist?... The freedom of the press was never understood to give the right of publishing falsehoods and slander, nor of exciting sedition, [rebellion], and slaughter.

The Results of the Alien and Sedition Acts

Jefferson said that the four new laws showed that the Federalists "mean to pay no respect" to the Constitution. Democratic-Republican papers attacked the laws, as well, and Democratic-Republican politicians saw the Sedition Act as a Federalist attempt to keep control of the government in the 1800 election. The law would, in theory, make Democratic-Republicans less able to point out flaws in Federalist policies.

After their passage, two of the alien laws had limited effect. Although the United States and France attacked each other's ships for almost two years, they never formally declared war on each other. Since the Alien Enemies Act only applied during a declared war, Adams never had a chance to use it. He also never used the Alien Friends Act. The law on citizenship did have some effect on reducing the number of immigrants who became U.S. citizens, though in 1801, Congress moved the waiting period for citizenship back to five years.

CHAPTER THREE

The Election of 1800

WHAT
A disputed election marks the first switch in power from one U.S. political party to another.

ISSUES
Federalist versus Democratic-Republican values; personal disagreements between politicians from the opposing parties

WHERE
Nationwide

WHEN
1800–1801

In his first speech as president, Thomas Jefferson called the election of 1800 a "contest of opinion." The election of 1800 featured strong opinions on both political issues and the candidates' personalities. In the end, the results preserved the peaceful transfer of power in the young government created by the U.S. Constitution.

The political feud between the first two U.S. political parties, the Federalists and the Democratic-Republicans, developed during the 1790s. Alexander Hamilton, a former secretary of the treasury, led the Federalists. They supported the strongest possible national government and expanding trade and industry. In foreign affairs, they were pro-British and feared the power of France. Jefferson was the leading Democratic-Republican. His party was against giving the national government too much power. Democratic-Republicans supported the country's farming interests and favored keeping good relations with France.

As the eighteenth century drew to a close, the conflict between the Federalist and the Democratic-Republican political parties was outdone only by the disputes within the Federalist Party itself. Alexander Hamilton, pictured here, was a former secretary of the treasury and leading Federalist who represented one of the factions within the party.

In 1798, under Federalist president John Adams, the battle between the two parties had turned especially ugly. While the country was fighting an undeclared war with France, the Federalists passed four laws known as the Alien and Sedition Acts. The laws, the Federalists claimed, were designed to strengthen the government and protect the country from enemies during a time of crisis. In reality, most of the laws were designed to limit the political power and influence of the Democratic-Republicans.

The following year, the Federalists began to argue among themselves. Adams hoped to use diplomacy to improve relations with France. This decision upset Hamilton and other Federalists, who strongly feared and hated the French. Hamilton began to speak out against Adams, and the president removed two members of his cabinet who supported Hamilton.

John Adams, pictured here, was a Federalist. He was president when the rift in his party developed in 1799. Opposing Alexander Hamilton, Adams removed two members of his own cabinet who supported Hamilton's policies.

> **Fast Fact**
>
> In 1798, John Adams named George Washington commander in chief of an expanded U.S. Army. Washington then made Hamilton his top aide—against Adams's wishes. Adams, however, felt that he had to accept Washington's choice for political reasons. This incident fueled Adam's anger toward Hamilton.

Thanks to Adams's diplomacy, the threat of a war with France faded. At the same time, the division between Federalists who disliked Adams and those who supported him grew. One Federalist wrote, "There is a decided and deep disgust with Mr. Adams on the part of his best old friends." The Democratic-Republican Party realized that it had a chance to do well in the 1800 election. In March of that year, Jefferson wrote to James Madison, another leading Democratic-Republican, "The Feds. begin to be very seriously alarmed about their election next fall."

The Election of 1800

During the election, each party chose two men to run for president and vice president. Under the system at the time, either candidate could be chosen for either position, but party leaders let their electors know who was the preferred choice for president. Despite the rising opposition to Adams among the Federalists, he remained his party's choice for president. The vice presidential candidate was Charles Cotesworth Pinckney of South Carolina. The Democratic-Republicans chose Jefferson as their presidential candidate and Aaron Burr of New York for vice president.

Under the laws of the era, the states had different methods for choosing electors, and the elections took place at different times. In ten states, the state legislators chose the electors. The party that controlled the state government could choose electors who would support its presidential candidate. In the remaining six states, the voters directly chose the electors.

By law, each state had to choose its electors by December 3. Once they were chosen, the electors cast their votes. Each elector had two votes. Federalist party leaders told all their electors to vote for Adams, while all but one should vote for Pinckney. This guaranteed that the results for the two men would not be tied.

The Democratic-Republicans issued the same instructions to their electors regarding their candidates, but something went wrong. When the final results came in, Jefferson and Burr both had seventy-three votes, Adams had sixty-five, and Pinckney had sixty-four. The Democratic-Republicans had won, but no one knew which man would be president.

ELECTORS AND THE ELECTORAL COLLEGE

In the United States, voters only indirectly choose their president. In each state, the political parties select electors who will vote for their party's candidate in the electoral college. This "college" has nothing to do with school—it is the meeting of the electors who actually choose the president. On Election Day, the votes for a particular candidate in each state decide which party's electors will represent the state in the electoral college. The number of electors from each state is the same as the state's total number of representatives and senators in Congress. The number of representatives is based on a state's population. Therefore, presidential candidates often focus on winning votes in the states with the largest populations, since they have more electoral votes. It is possible for a candidate to win more individual votes across the country—the popular vote—and still lose in the electoral college. This last happened in 2000, when Republican George W. Bush beat Democrat Al Gore.

Breaking the Tie

Under the Constitution, the U.S. House of Representatives breaks a tie between two presidential candidates. Each state has one vote, decided by a vote among its representatives. If one party in a state has more representatives than the other, that party's candidate usually receives the single state vote. If the representatives from one state have a tie vote, that state's vote is not counted.

Fast Fact
The 1800 presidential election marked the first time that Congress met in Washington, D.C., to count electoral votes. In 1789, the capital had been in New York City, and for the next two elections it was in Philadelphia, Pennsylvania.

In February 1801, the House met to choose the next president. Its members at the time were part of the Sixth Congress. The new Seventh Congress would take office on the same day as the new president, March 4. The Democratic-Republicans controlled the new Congress, but the Federalists had a majority in the Sixth Congress. They could disrupt the Democratic-Republicans' plan to have Jefferson serve as president. Jefferson wrote to James Monroe, the governor of Virginia, "We remain in the hands of our enemies." Jefferson and his supporters worried that the Federalists would choose Burr. To many Federalists, Burr was the least offensive of the two Democratic-Republican candidates.

When the voting began, Jefferson managed to win eight states—one less than he needed to become president. Several days passed as the representatives went through thirty-six rounds of voting. Finally, on February 17, Federalists from Maryland and Vermont agreed not to vote. The Democratic-Republicans from those two states then voted for Jefferson, giving him a total of ten state votes—and the presidency.

> **Fast Fact**
>
> The First Congress met in 1789. Every two years, as members are elected to Congress, the number of the congressional session increases by one.

The Federalists' Issues

In their efforts to defeat Jefferson, Hamilton and other Federalists focused on several issues. As in the past, they accused Jefferson of being too close to the government in France. Jefferson had supported the French Revolution (1789–1799) even when it had turned increasingly violent during the 1790s.

The revolutionary French government had weakened the power of the Roman Catholic Church in France, and many Americans considered the French to be enemies of religion. Jefferson, by association, was also condemned for being against Christianity, the dominant American religion. Ministers spoke out against him, calling him an atheist—someone who does not believe in any god.

While attacking Jefferson, Hamilton was also trying to weaken support for Adams. The Federalist leader hoped to secretly win support for Pinckney. In October, Hamilton passed around a letter to some Federalists. It said that Adams had "great...defects" that made him unfit to hold the presidency. The letter became public, making Adams look foolish to many people. However, Hamilton was also attacked since he said such harsh words about the man representing his party in the election. Adams still had supporters in the party, and the Federalists remained split through the election.

Once the election moved into the House of Representatives, the Federalists debated a new issue: whom to support for president. For most Federalists, the answer was clear: Burr. Hamilton, however, despite his dislike of Jefferson and his beliefs, also opposed Burr. The political struggles between Burr and Hamilton in New York fed each man's hatred for the other. The Federalists once again split, as many ignored Hamilton's views and tried to make Burr president. One Virginia Federalist, John Marshall, thought that Jefferson's pro-French views made him unfit to be president. "I cannot bring myself to aid Mr. Jefferson," Marshall wrote.

> *Fast Fact*
>
> In January 1801, before the House vote on the election, John Adams named John Marshall the chief justice of the Supreme Court. Marshall helped develop the idea of judicial review—that the court could decide if laws were or were not allowed under the Constitution.

In Their Own Words

Here is part of a letter that Hamilton wrote attacking Burr's character and trying to convince other Federalists to support Jefferson.

He knows well the weak sides of human nature and takes care to play in with the passions of all with whom he [deals].... He will...employ able and daring young scoundrels of every party and...attempt [a government takeover]. No mortal can tell what his political principles are.... If he has any theory, 'tis that of simple despotism.

The Democratic-Republicans' Issues

In the 1800 campaign, Jefferson and the Democratic-Republicans targeted three main issues. The undeclared war with France had led to the creation of a standing army in the United States—a national army that was always in place. Since colonial days, many Americans had disliked the idea of a standing army. They associated such an army with the British, who had limited their freedoms in the years before the American Revolution. The Democratic-Republicans tried to suggest that a U.S. standing army could also be used to threaten individual rights. Jefferson had spoken out against standing armies for years, saying that they were "inconsistent with [a people's] freedom." He and other Democratic-Republicans continued to spread that message in 1800.

Taxes were another key Democratic-Republican issue. Adams had raised taxes in 1798 to pay for a growing navy and the army. The taxes were based on the amount of property that a person owned. Jefferson argued that the government should be kept small so that taxes could be cut. He also wanted to reduce the national debt, the amount of money that the country owed when it spent more than it earned. The debt had risen under Adams. Jefferson believed that a high debt forced the government to raise taxes, which took money away from citizens.

The third major issue for the Democratic-Republicans was the Sedition Act. This 1798 law made it illegal to criticize government officials and their actions or weaken public support for the government. Jefferson had opposed the law from the beginning. Several Democratic-Republican newspaper editors had been arrested under the Sedition Act. Democratic-Republicans cited the law as another Federalist limit on American freedom.

Once the campaign was over, the Democratic-Republicans faced a new issue: how to respond to the tie vote between

Jefferson and Burr. Some Democratic-Republicans feared that the Federalists would somehow use the tie vote as an excuse for keeping the presidency. One Democratic-Republican member of Congress said that "Virginia would instantly proclaim herself out of the Union" if the Federalists tried to "steal" the election. Another Democratic-Republican leader suggested that their party members in Congress should simply refuse to work with the Federalists if they tried any illegal action.

Some Democratic-Republicans also seemed split over whom to support for president. A few considered switching their vote from Jefferson to Burr if that were the only way to keep the Federalists out of power. In the end, however, the Democratic-Republicans remained united behind Jefferson.

During the election crisis of 1800, some Americans worried that the country was heading toward civil war. Jefferson later referred to the result as the "revolution of 1800." The country had gone through a drastic political change by going from the Federalists to the Democratic-Republicans. Despite all the problems in settling the election, the country had avoided violence and survived the conflict. Jefferson hoped that the bad feelings created during the election could be put aside so that Federalists and Democratic-Republicans could work together. Debates between the two parties, however, continued for years to come.

A MORE VIOLENT OPTION

Thomas McKean, the Democratic-Republican governor of Pennsylvania, had another plan for stopping the Federalists from illegally taking power. If the Federalists claimed the presidency, he was going to order all Pennsylvania state officials to accept orders only from Jefferson or Burr. Then McKean planned to arm 20,000 militia troops and arrest anyone who helped the Federalists. McKean never discussed the details of his plan until after Jefferson's election.

Thomas Jefferson.

In Their Own Words

At their inaugural—the ceremony that officially makes them president—U.S. presidents always give a speech. Here is part of Jefferson's inauguration speech after the election of 1800.

[This election] now being decided by the voice of the nation...all will, of course, arrange themselves under the will of the law, and unite in common efforts for the common good.... Let us then, fellow citizens, unite with one heart and one mind.... Let us, then, with courage and confidence pursue our own Federal and Republican principles, our attachment to union and representative government.

CHAPTER FOUR

The Louisiana Purchase

WHAT
The United States purchases territory from France.

ISSUES
The constitutionality of the purchase;
the governing of the new territory

WHERE
New Orleans and French territory west of the Mississippi River

WHEN
1803–1804

With its victory in the American Revolution (1775–1783), the United States took control of former British lands east of the Mississippi River. Many Americans realized that the river would play an important role for the new country, moving goods and people from states along the river down to the Gulf of Mexico. Settlers also eyed land west of the river for future expansion. That region, known as Louisiana, was under Spanish control at the time.

Starting in 1784, Spain tried to deny Americans access to the Mississippi River. It refused to let U.S. ships use New Orleans, the major port at the mouth of the river. Finally, in 1788, the Spanish agreed to let the Americans use New Orleans for a fee. Still, some western settlers thought that they might be better off breaking away from the United States and becoming part of Spanish Louisiana to ensure access to the river.

While serving as U.S. ambassador to France, Thomas Jefferson closely followed the events in the western United States. He was one of many U.S. leaders who saw the future value of the Mississippi River and the lands west of it. His focus on expansion grew after he became president in 1801. That year, he wrote, "It is impossible not to look forward to distant times when our multiplication will expand...and cover the whole northern if not the southern continent."

LOUISIANA

The Louisiana Territory covered a large portion of the land between the Mississippi River and the Rocky Mountains, from the Gulf of Mexico to what is now the Canadian border. French Louisiana had once included lands east of the Mississippi, but they had come under British rule after the French and Indian War (1754–1763). In the mid-eighteenth century, control of the territory switched from France to Spain.

The Louisiana Purchase of 1803 virtually doubled the size of the United States. This map also shows other land acquisitions that were made around the same time.

Foreign Politics and Louisiana

When Jefferson took office, changes were taking shape in Louisiana. In September 1800, Spain secretly agreed to give Louisiana back to France, in exchange for land that France controlled in Italy. Louisiana had become too expensive for the Spanish, who spent more money running the territory than they earned from it. France was eager to regain its former colony. France's ruler, Napoleon Bonaparte, wanted to create a powerful French empire. Farms in Louisiana would provide food and supplies to French plantations on islands that France owned in the Caribbean Sea.

France and Spain did not announce their trade for almost two years. In the meantime, Jefferson heard rumors of the deal. Just before he took office, the United States and France had ended an undeclared naval war that had gone on for two years. Jefferson worried that Napoleon could not be trusted to keep good relations with America. The president feared that the French might someday cut off American access to the Mississippi

River and limit U.S. efforts to expand westward. He also worried that western settlers might start a war by taking over New Orleans and parts of Florida before the French took control.

Jefferson preferred that Louisiana stay with Spain, and he asked Great Britain to try to influence the French to stop the deal. However, Great Britain and France were just ending a war with each other. The British did not want to get involved in France's affairs in North America. In addition, some British leaders wanted the Americans to feel threatened by France. This would make the United States reliant on British help in the future. The British preferred to see the United States stay as weak as possible.

As American fears and anger grew, Jefferson wrote that "every eye in the U.S. is now fixed on this affair of Louisiana. Perhaps nothing since the revolutionary war has produced more uneasy sensations through the body of the nation."

Famous Figures

NAPOLEON BONAPARTE
(1769–1821)

At the end of the eighteenth century, there was a revolution in France. The French Revolution (1789–1799) ended royal rule in that country. After several years of violence and different governments, Napoleon Bonaparte emerged as the leader of France. Born on the French island of Corsica, he became a general in the revolutionary army when he was twenty-five. In 1799, he took command of the government, and five years later, he named himself emperor of France. On the battlefield, he won many victories as France took control of large parts of Europe. Under Napoleon's rule, France fought a series of wars with Great Britain. During these Napoleonic Wars (1799–1815), both France and Great Britain sometimes seized U.S. ships. This practice eventually led to the War of 1812 (1812–1815) between the Americans and the British.

Making a Deal

During 1802, American leaders saw a way to prevent any possible war and take control of New Orleans. The country offered to buy the port and part of West Florida in 1803.

At the same time, France was facing trouble in Saint-Domingue (present-day Haiti), its major colony in the Caribbean. A former slave named François Dominique Toussaint L'Ouverture had led a slave rebellion and taken control of the colony, located on the island of Hispaniola. In 1802, a huge French military force arrived in Saint-Domingue to restore French rule. The fighting went poorly for the French, and by spring 1803, Napoleon realized that he could not regain the colony. Without Saint-Domingue, France no longer needed the supplies that Louisiana could provide.

Napoleon was also preparing for another war with Great Britain, and he needed money to fund the effort. Knowing of the American offer, Napoleon told an aide, "It is not only New Orleans I cede; it is the whole colony, without reserve." For $15 million, the United States received all of the Louisiana Territory. Technically, West Florida was not part of the territory, but the treaty allowed the Americans to make a claim on it.

Most Americans supported the Louisiana Purchase, though some, including Jefferson, wondered if the deal was legal. The U.S. Constitution did not state that the president or Congress had the power to buy territory for the country. In most cases, Jefferson thought that the government should do only what the Constitution specifically said that it could do. He wrote to one cabinet member that the Constitution "has not given [the government] a power of holding foreign territory, and still less of incorporating it into the Union." For a time, Jefferson thought that he should call for an amendment to the Constitution to give the government that power.

> *Fast Fact*
> During colonial times, Florida was split into two colonies—East and West Florida. Great Britain won them from Spain at the end of the French and Indian War and then gave them back to Spain at the end of the American Revolution. France sought part of West Florida when it took back Louisiana.

In the fall, Congress approved the treaty and set aside money for running the new U.S. territory. At the time, Spain still had troops in New Orleans and the southern portion of Louisiana. On November 30, 1803, Spain peacefully turned over control of Louisiana to France, and about three weeks later the French gave southern Louisiana to the Americans. The transfer of the northern half of the territory took place a few months later.

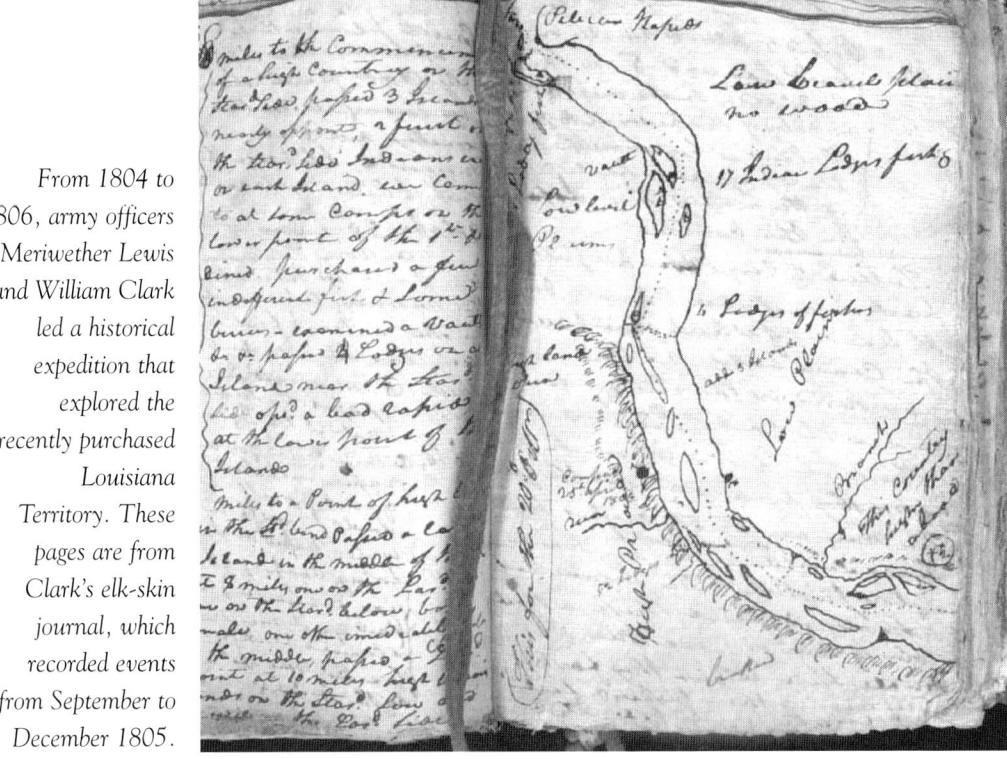

From 1804 to 1806, army officers Meriwether Lewis and William Clark led a historical expedition that explored the recently purchased Louisiana Territory. These pages are from Clark's elk-skin journal, which recorded events from September to December 1805.

Opposition to the Louisiana Purchase

Jefferson's political enemies strongly opposed the Louisiana Purchase. Jefferson belonged to the Democratic-Republican Party. The Democratic-Republicans' opponents, the Federalists, attacked the purchase in the press and in Congress.

In general, the Federalists received most of their support from New Englanders and people who lived along the eastern seaboard. Many Federalists were involved in shipping and commerce. The Democratic-Republicans drew their main support from farmers, particularly in the southern and western states. The Federalists believed that any new states carved out of Louisiana would be settled mostly by farmers, who would likely vote Democratic-Republican.

In public, the Federalists raised several points to question the purchase. If the United States expanded westward, the Federalists claimed, the government would not run as efficiently as it did in a smaller region. In addition, the western settlers would lose contact with the commercial and cultural centers of the East. "They will gradually begin to view us as strangers," said Federalist senator Samuel White. Some Federalists questioned the value of the land and thought that the country was paying too much for it. Some also raised the questions that Jefferson had raised about whether or not the deal was allowed under the Constitution.

When the Federalists' arguments did not stop the purchase, Jefferson's critics found another issue to debate. They attacked the way that the new territory would be ruled. On this issue, some Democratic-Republicans joined Federalists in criticizing the government's position. Jefferson wanted to restrict democracy in Louisiana, because he did not think that the French and Spanish citizens there were ready for self-rule. The people in Louisiana would not have the freedom to run their own political affairs, as Americans did in other western territories. Critics said that the plan set up a despotic government that went against American ideals. They also accused Democratic-Republicans of going against their own beliefs. Just a few years before, they had accused Federalist president John Adams of ruling like a tyrant. Now, one Federalist said, the Democratic-Republicans were making "the modest Jefferson despot of Louisiana."

> *Fast Fact*
> Not all Federalists opposed the Louisiana Purchase. Some welcomed westward expansion and the acquisition of new lands. The Federalists who opposed Jefferson were mostly from New England.

In Their Owns Words

Here is part of a speech that Samuel White of Delaware made opposing the Louisiana Purchase.

We have already territory enough, and when I contemplate the evils that may arise to these states from this intended [purchase] of Louisiana...I would rather see it given to France, to Spain, or to any other nation of the earth....

...And I do say that under existing circumstances, even supposing that this extent of territory was a desirable acquisition, $15 million was a most enormous sum to give.

Defense of the Louisiana Purchase

Supporters of the Louisiana Purchase said that the deal guaranteed American access to the Mississippi River and New Orleans. It also removed any future threat from France in North America. Democratic-Republican senator John Breckinridge of Kentucky attacked the notion that an expanded republic would not function well. He argued that "the more extensive" the country was, "the more safe and durable it will be."

In general, the Democratic-Republicans shared Jefferson's belief in the value of farmers and agriculture to the country. Jefferson saw that the new land would allow more people to own their own farms. He believed that farming was better for the country than building large cities and factories. Farmers, he believed, helped keep a republican government strong.

Democratic-Republicans also argued that the purchase was legal under the Constitution, since the document did not specifically say that the government could not buy new lands. Thomas

Paine wrote that the purchase "makes no alteration in the Constitution, it only extends the principles of it over a larger territory, and this certainly is within the morality of the Constitution."

As far as governing Louisiana, Jefferson believed that the French and Spanish citizens there were not ready for self-rule. The region lacked good schools, and the people had no experience with the American legal and political system. However, James Madison said the people of Louisiana would receive "every blessing of liberty...as fast as they shall be prepared...to receive it."

Most Americans of the era favored westward expansion, and the Louisiana Purchase was one of the highlights of Jefferson's presidency. Through peaceful means, Jefferson nearly doubled the size of the United States.

Support for the Louisiana Purchase was divided mainly along political-party lines. In this negative cartoon President Jefferson is pictured as a prairie dog coughing up $2 million as Napoleon dances around waving maps in front of him.

A NEW HOMELAND?

In addition to farming, Thomas Jefferson saw another use for western lands. He thought that the government should set aside some of it for Native American tribes who lived east of the Mississippi. The tribes would be resettled in the West, and their old lands could then be sold to Americans. This policy of "Indian removal" started during the 1830s. Tens of thousands of Native Americans were forced off their lands and resettled in what is now Oklahoma and parts of Arkansas, Kansas, and Nebraska.

In Their Own Words

On October 17, 1803, Thomas Jefferson delivered his State of the Union address to Congress. Here is some of what he said about the Louisiana Purchase.

While the property and sovereignty of the Mississippi and its waters secure an independent outlet for the produce of the western States, and an uncontrolled navigation through their whole course, free from collision with other powers and the dangers to our peace from that source, the fertility of the country, its climate and extent, promise in due season important aids to our treasury...and a wide-spread field for the blessings of freedom and equal laws.

CHAPTER FIVE

The Burr Conspiracy

WHAT
Aaron Burr is accused of treason and found innocent.

ISSUES
*A president's right not to appear in court;
the legal definition of treason; Burr's guilt*

WHERE
Richmond, Virginia

WHEN
1807

During his life, Aaron Burr was a controversial figure, and he remains one today. In 1800, Burr was almost elected president of the United States. Four years later, while serving as vice president, he shot and killed Alexander Hamilton in a duel. Shortly after the duel, Burr came up with a plan to take part of Mexico from Spain, which controlled the region at the time. His plan also seemed to include convincing Americans in western lands to break off from the United States and form a new country with Mexico.

Burr's conspiracy unfolded while Thomas Jefferson was president. Both men belonged to the Democratic-Republican Party. In 1800, Jefferson was the party's choice for the presidency, but the election resulted in a tie between him and Burr. The election was finally decided by a special vote in the U.S. House of Representatives, giving Jefferson the presidency and Burr the vice presidency. Burr knew that he was not the party's choice for the presidency, but he never pulled out of the vote so that Jefferson could win. The results led to distrust between the president and Burr, and Jefferson and the Democratic-Republicans did not name him as the vice presidential candidate in 1804.

Burr also had a long history of conflict with Hamilton. The former secretary of the treasury, Hamilton led the Federalists, the other major political party of the era. Burr and Hamilton were both from New York, and they competed for political power there. In the 1800 presidential election, Hamilton supported Jefferson, even though he opposed many of Jefferson's political beliefs. Hamilton believed that Burr would be more dangerous to the government. He wrote, "Mr. Burr loves nothing but himself—thinks of nothing but his own [advancement]—and will be content with nothing short of permanent power."

THE DUEL

The hatred between Burr and Hamilton led to bloodshed in 1804. Burr accused Hamilton of insulting him, which was a continuation of Hamilton's long assault on his character. Hamilton refused to admit that he had made an attack on Burr, and Burr challenged him to a duel. Dueling was illegal in New York at the time, so the two men met on July 11 in Weehawken, New Jersey. Each man held a pistol. Hamilton fired his into the air; the bullet was later found in a tree. Historians are not sure if Hamilton deliberately tried to miss Burr or if he missed by accident. Burr's shot hit Hamilton in the stomach, and the next day, Hamilton died from his wound. Burr fled New Jersey, as he was now wanted for murder. Despite the charge against him, Burr continued his duties as vice president.

A portrayal of the duel between Aaron Burr and Alexander Hamilton on July 11, 1804, at Weehawken, New Jersey.

> ### *Famous Figures*
>
> ## AARON BURR
> ## (1756–1836)
>
> Aaron Burr came from a well-respected New Jersey family. Burr studied at the College of New Jersey (present-day Princeton University) before fighting in the American Revolution (1775–1783). After the war, Burr settled in New York and began a successful legal and political career. His goal of seizing territory from Mexico led to his being put on trial for conspiracy. After his legal troubles ended in 1807, Burr lived in Europe for a time and then returned to his law practice in New York in 1812.

Visions of Empire

In 1805, with his term as vice president over, Burr left Washington, D.C., for Pittsburgh, Pennsylvania. He had already discussed with several friends his idea to raise an army, seize Mexico, and perhaps take control of parts of the western United States. Burr also wanted British aid to carry out his plan.

At the time, Great Britain was at war with Spain and France. The United States had recently purchased Louisiana from France. Bordering Louisiana were Mexico and Florida, both owned by Spain. The British seemed eager to weaken Spain by helping Burr take Mexico. But, Spain did not want to lose any territory in North America. Some Americans thought that the United States might go to war with Spain, and the United States kept a military force in New Orleans, the major city in Louisiana.

General James Wilkinson was the commander of the U.S. troops in Louisiana. He also served as governor of part of the territory. He and Burr had served together during the American Revolution. Burr told Wilkinson about his military plans for Mexico and the West, and Wilkinson pledged his support. Through the summer of 1805, Burr traveled

> *Fast Fact*
>
> In 1806, Congress set aside $2 million to buy Florida from Spain, but the deal never took place. Most of Florida did not become part of the United States until 1819.

across the country, discussing his plans. Rumors of his plans spread everywhere. Still, without hard facts, the government could not take action against Burr, and he continued to recruit assistants and gather supplies for his planned attack.

By the fall of 1806, Burr had created a small army and was ready to attack. Wilkinson, however, had decided that he did not want to be part of the conspiracy. He wrote to Jefferson, warning him of the plan. At this point, Jefferson issued a public statement, telling Americans in the West not to attack Spanish territory. Spain and the United States were not at war, and an attack on Mexico would violate a U.S. law known as the Neutrality Act. Anyone who violated the act faced arrest. Jefferson did not mention Burr by name or hint that there was any kind of plan to take over U.S. territory in the West, but the president wanted to charge Burr with committing treason for his role in the conspiracy.

Into the Courtroom

Jefferson's warning caused some of Burr's recruits to abandon the plot to attack Mexico. Still, in December, a small group of the recruits met on an island in the Ohio River to begin a voyage south. Burr was not there, but by the end of the month, he met up with the force.

When people along Burr's route south found out that he was a wanted man, local militia came after him and his supporters. Burr tried to get away, but in January 1807, he was caught in Mississippi. He escaped and went into hiding, but he was caught again and brought to Richmond, Virginia, to face trial.

The government charged that Burr had committed treason by "assembling an armed force, with designs to seize the city of New Orleans,...revolutionize the territory attached to it,...and separate the western from the Atlantic states." The judge hearing the case was Chief Justice John Marshall of the U.S. Supreme

> *Fast Fact*
> One of the men that Burr recruited was Jonathan Dayton, a former U.S. senator from New Jersey. The city of Dayton, Ohio, is named for him.

Court. In the end, Marshall ruled that the court had not proved Burr's guilt. In a second trial, Burr was also found innocent of breaking the Neutrality Act for his planned invasion of Mexico.

> **TREASON AND THE CONSTITUTION**
> In the U.S. Constitution, treason is the only crime specifically defined, with instructions on how it must be proved in court. Article III, Section 3, says, "Treason against the United States shall consist only in levying war against them, or in adhering to their enemies, giving them aid and comfort." To prove treason, the government had to present two witnesses to an overt, or open, treasonous act, or the accused had to confess.

The First Legal Battle

Before the actual trial, Burr appeared before a grand jury. Its job was to decide if the government had enough evidence to charge Burr with treason. Burr wanted to see what information Jefferson had on the case, including a letter that he had received from Wilkinson. In that letter, Wilkinson quoted from a letter that he said he had received from Burr. In it, Burr supposedly said, "I have...obtained funds, and have actually commenced." He went on to describe the plan for attacking Mexico. Wilkinson also reported on plans that he had heard from one of Burr's aides.

Burr's lawyers made a legal request, or subpoena, for Jefferson to come to court with the government documents. The government's lawyers said that Burr's lawyers would get copies of official documents, but that the court could not force Jefferson to turn over private papers. Justice Marshall told both teams of lawyers to prepare arguments on the issue, and then he would decide if Jefferson's papers could be subpoenaed.

Fast Fact
Before Burr's trial, Jefferson told the public that he had no doubt that Burr was guilty of treason. This statement went against the American legal notion of a person being innocent until proven guilty.

The government's lawyers claimed that Jefferson, as the president, had special demands. He was too busy to appear in court, and his papers might include information that might harm the government if it was revealed. They also said that Burr did not have a right to ask for the papers until he was actually charged with a crime. At times, the arguments became personal attacks on Burr—one government lawyer said that Burr would have been better off killed when he was on the run if he had, in fact, "placed himself in a state of war with his country."

Burr's lawyers said that the government was trying to claim Jefferson was above the law. "Even the British king," attorney Luther Martin said, "may be called upon to give testimony to his people." Martin also reminded the court that Jefferson had already said that Burr was guilty, and now Jefferson would not provide evidence that might help Burr's case.

> **Fast Fact**
> A president's claim to keep certain documents private is called executive privilege. In general, the U.S. Supreme Court has not allowed presidents the right to withhold all requested information during criminal trials.

After several days of heated arguments, Marshall reached his decision. Under the Constitution, he said, the president did not have any special right to deny the subpoena. Some papers, the judge realized, might have information that should not be revealed in public, but he would decide on that once the papers were in court. Burr had won his first legal victory.

What Is Treason?

In the end, the grand jury decided there was enough evidence to bring Burr to trial. The government then tried to prove that he had committed treason, as it is defined in the Constitution. Burr said that he was innocent. The government argued that Burr was the brains behind the plot, even though he had not been present when his "army" first set sail in December 1806. The lawyers also argued that plotting treason alone was a crime, even if Burr had not committed an overt act.

Justice Marshall had heard an earlier case involving one of the men involved in the Burr conspiracy. At that time, he had said that if a group of men met to levy (wage) war against the government, "all those who perform any part...however remote from the scene of action...are to be considered as traitors." The government lawyers said that ruling applied in Burr's case.

The government brought in witnesses who said that Burr had talked about committing treason—seizing control of western lands belonging to the United States—but no one had actually seen him committing treason. The witnesses also described the group of Burr's supporters that had met in December 1806 to begin the journey to Mexico. Some had guns—a sign, the lawyers said, that they were going to use force and levy war. Even though Burr had not been there, he was part of the plot, and therefore guilty.

Burr's lawyers attacked this claim. One of them, John Wickham, noted that the Constitution was clear about how to define treason. No one had seen Burr commit an overt act of treason, "and no overt act of others can, under the [law], be made his overt act."

On August 31, Marshall reached his decision. To commit treason, Burr had to be connected with actual military force used against the government. Burr's supporters, even though they had weapons, had not used actual force. Even if they had, two witnesses had to show that Burr had played a part in employing that force. Even the government said that Burr had not been present when his supporters met in Ohio, and none of the witnesses said that Burr ordered his supporters to meet on an island with weapons. Therefore, Marshall said, Burr had not committed an overt act or taken part in using actual force against the United States. The next day, the jury found Burr not guilty.

Fast Fact

During the early 1800s, Supreme Court justices traveled to federal courts called circuit courts. This job was in addition to their duties in Washington, D.C., with the Supreme Court. Marshall heard Burr's case as part of his circuit court duties.

Famous Figures

JOHN MARSHALL
(1755–1835)

John Marshall was a distant cousin of Thomas Jefferson. Despite their family ties, the two men were bitter political enemies. Marshall was a dedicated Federalist who believed that Jefferson sought too much power as president.

Marshall fought in the American Revolution. Like Burr, he spent the winter of 1777–1778 at Valley Forge, though the two men did not seem to know each other there. After the war, Marshall studied law and started a successful practice in Virginia. In 1797, President John Adams sent Marshall to France on a diplomatic mission. Four years later, the president made him chief justice of the Supreme Court. Marshall is considered one of the greatest chief justices in U.S. history. He held the position until his death, writing the decisions for more than 500 cases. One of the most important was for *Marbury v. Madison*. In that case, for the first time, the court declared that a law passed by Congress was unconstitutional. In the future, the court would continue to determine if laws were allowed under the Constitution.

In Their Own Words

Here is part of a speech given in court by Luther Martin, one of Aaron Burr's attorneys.

Though [treason] is said to be here and there and everywhere, yet it is nowhere. It exists only in the newspapers and in the mouths of the enemies of the gentleman for whom I appear.... I have...heard it said that such are the public prejudices against Colonel Burr that a jury, even should they be satisfied of his innocence, must have considerable firmness of mind to pronounce him not guilty.

In Their Own Words

Here is part of a speech given by William Wirt, one of the government lawyers in the trial against Aaron Burr.

Pervading the continent from New York to New Orleans, he draws into his plan, by every [temptation possible], men of all ranks and descriptions.... To each person whom he addresses he presents the object adapted to his taste. His recruiting officers are appointed. Men are engaged throughout the continent. Civil life is indeed quiet upon its surface; but in its [heart] this man has contrived to...produce an explosion to shake the continent.

Was Burr Guilty?

Burr proclaimed that he was innocent of treason, and technically this was true, given the definition of treason in the Constitution and Marshall's views on it. However, Americans at the time were not sure if Burr had really planned to break off the western states from the Union. A key piece of evidence against him was the coded letter that he supposedly had sent to James Wilkinson. In court, Wilkinson admitted that he had forged some of the letter. Historians now believe that Burr did not write any of the coded letter that suggested his plan for conquest was under way.

Aaron Burr is defended in court during his 1807 trial for treason. The trial helped shape the legal definition of treason, which involves using force against one's own country. It was convincingly argued that since Burr had not been seen committing any act of treason, he should not be found guilty. Indeed, Burr was found to be innocent.

Public opinion was split on Burr. In 1806, crowds in Kentucky cheered him after a grand jury refused to bring charges against him. By the time of Burr's Richmond trial, however, the government attorneys believed that most Americans suspected he was guilty. Still, one reporter at the trial, Washington Irving, wrote that the ladies of Richmond "would but rejoice in seeing Colonel Burr at liberty."

The charges against Burr in Kentucky came from local Federalists who opposed him. Federalist newspapers also spread rumors about the conspiracy, hoping to taint the Democratic-Republican Party. Yet not all Federalists thought that Burr was guilty. In February 1807, John Adams, the former president and a Federalist, said that a "lying spirit has been at work concerning Burr." A Federalist reporter wrote that he was "an unbeliever in the truth of the principle charges against the said Burr."

In charging Burr with treason, President Jefferson seemed to be carrying out a personal attack on Burr. Even Jefferson sometimes admitted that he didn't know for sure if Burr were guilty. Jefferson wrote to one U.S. diplomat that Burr had first planned to break off the western states, "yet he very early saw that the fidelity of the western country was not to be shaken, and turned himself wholly towards Mexico."

No one knows exactly what Burr said or wrote to the people that he recruited for his conspiracy. Some people still believe that he planned to make himself the ruler of a new country west of the Appalachian Mountains. Others insist that politics and personal feelings against him led to his famous trial.

CHAPTER SIX

The Embargo of 1808

WHAT
Congress passes a series of laws that limit U.S. foreign trade.

ISSUES
The legality and desirability of the laws

WHERE
Nationwide

WHEN
1808–1809

Starting in the early 1790s, Great Britain and France fought a series of wars that lasted until 1815. These wars in Europe often affected the United States. In 1793, President Washington said that the country would remain neutral. Americans, however, showed strong feelings for or against the British and the French. The United States sometimes even seemed prepared to go to war against either France or Great Britain. Each country often captured American merchant vessels carrying goods to its enemy.

In the early 1800s, American ships were carrying large amounts of goods to France and its ally, Spain. Often, the ships stopped first at an American port as they traveled between European ports and French and Spanish colonies in the Caribbean Sea. This extra stop created what was called "a broken voyage." The stop was necessary to get around a British policy that prevented direct trade between France and its colonies on neutral ships. Neutral ships carrying on direct trade were stopped by British warships. The British then took the goods for themselves.

In 1805, a British court ruled that many American ships were violating the policy against direct trade, even though they made a stop in the United States. The shippers were not dropping off foreign goods in the United States or bringing American goods to Europe. The broken voyage was merely a deceitful way to avoid the British policy against direct trade. The British began seizing ships making broken voyages, which threatened to harm U.S. trade with France and Spain.

At times, British ships anchored off the Atlantic coast of the United States, waiting to board U.S. merchant ships that violated Britain's policy. In one incident, a British ship fired a cannonball past a merchant ship leaving New York City. The ball ripped into another American ship nearby, killing a sailor. The British apologized, but many New Yorkers were upset by the accident.

> *Fast Fact*
> From 1798 to 1800, U.S. and French ships sometimes fought each other. This military action was called a quasi-war, meaning that it resembled a war, even though the two nations did not officially declare war.

More Troubles at Sea

In 1806, the British announced a blockade around France and lands that the French controlled in Europe. British ships would prevent French ships from sailing and stop other nations' ships from reaching French ports. Later in the year, the French placed their own blockade around Great Britain. The United States protested both actions, saying that the blockades were not valid because neither European power had enough ships to actually enforce their blockades. Under international law, a country had to have ships actively patrolling to enforce a blockade. Despite the protest, the two European nations went on with their so-called paper blockades.

> **Fast Fact**
> As Great Britain and France fought their wars, U.S. ships carried an additional 70,000 tons (63,000 metric tons) of goods each year, trading with both nations and their allies.

To President Jefferson, a larger issue with the British was naval impressment. British sailors were often impressed—forced to serve in the navy. The British treated their sailors badly, giving them low pay and poor food. Sailors received much better treatment on American merchant ships, so many British sailors left their ships to work for the Americans. Since the 1790s, the British had been stopping American ships to look for British sailors who had deserted from the British navy. Claiming that some American sailors were actually British citizens, the British took them off the American ships and forced them to serve on British ships. Secretary of State James Madison stated that several thousand Americans had been impressed in this way. He called impressment an "authorized system of kidnapping upon the ocean."

The impressment issue became a crisis in June 1807. A British ship attacked the *Chesapeake*, a U.S. warship, after the *Chesapeake*'s captain refused to let the British board his ship to search for deserters. After a quick victory, the British came aboard and took off four supposed deserters. Three of the sailors were clearly American. Members of both major U.S. political parties, the Federalists and the Democratic-Republicans, denounced the attack. President Jefferson responded by closing American ports to British ships. He also hinted that the United States might invade Canada—a British colony at the time—if the British did not meet U.S. demands. These included paying for damages, punishing the British officers involved in the attack, and promising to end all impressments.

> ### FAILED TREATY TALKS
> During the 1790s, the United States and Great Britain had solved several disputes with a treaty negotiated by diplomat John Jay. In 1806, the Americans tried to use diplomacy again to settle their differences with the British. James Monroe, a future U.S. president, and William Pinkney, a lawyer from Maryland, carried out the negotiations. The treaty that they signed allowed U.S. ships to make broken voyages, but it did not force the British to end impressments. Jefferson rejected the treaty.

The Embargo Acts

Instead of agreeing to end impressments, as Jefferson demanded, the British announced that they would carry out more searches, including searches of U.S. warships. The British also created a new policy that would force Americans to pay a tax to trade with France or its allies. French leader Napoleon Bonaparte then said that his forces would seize any ships that paid the tax.

Great Britain's policies posed the most direct threat to U.S. interests, and many Americans called for a war against the British. Despite the tough talk, the United States lacked the military power to confront the British, and Jefferson was not eager to start a war. Still, Americans wanted some government response to the *Chesapeake* affair and harmful British policies.

Relying on the advice of Madison, Jefferson proposed an embargo on U.S. ships. No ships would be allowed to leave port and trade overseas. Madison wanted to prevent impressment from becoming an issue that would lead to war. He also believed that the embargo would prevent both Great Britain and France from receiving necessary food and supplies. Along with the embargo, Congress approved a law that stopped British goods from entering the United States.

In January 1808, Congress passed a second embargo act. This law required ships that sailed along the U.S. coast to pay money, called a bond, before leaving port. If they tried to break the embargo and sail overseas, the ships' owners lost the bond. Ship owners also faced other penalties if their ships were caught breaking the embargo. A third embargo act increased the penalties for breaking the embargo and also ended foreign trade over land routes.

While the United States was reluctant to declare war on Great Britain, most people wanted some kind of decisive reaction to Britain's attack on the warship Chesapeake, pictured above. The result was the four embargo acts. These acts succeeded in hindering trade with Great Britain, but they also hurt the U.S. economy.

With the third law, some Americans began to protest the embargo. New Englanders and New Yorkers, ignoring the law against land trade, took goods into Canada. Some shippers also ignored a requirement that they get permission from the government before sailing. Albert Gallatin, the secretary of the treasury, wrote that "we have not been properly supported by the people.... Love of gain...has rendered the stoppage of [trade]...unpopular."

The smuggling led Jefferson to demand a fourth embargo law. He asked for broad powers to enforce the other embargo acts. The new Enforcement Act let Jefferson call in the navy and army to stop the illegal movement of goods out of the country. The law also allowed government officials to seize cargo from ships if the officials suspected that the ships might try to break the embargo.

> *Fast Fact*
>
> Under the Embargo Acts, American ships could still carry goods between U.S. ports, and foreign ships could bring in goods from overseas.

Jefferson hoped that the embargo would prevent war, but it stirred angry reactions in parts of the United States. Some New Englanders even talked of leaving the Union, and other Americans did not like that the embargo had to be enforced under the threat of military violence. Even some members of Jefferson's party criticized the embargo. Finally, on March 1, 1809, Congress voted to end the embargo on March 4—the day that Jefferson would leave the presidency. In its place, Congress passed a law that prohibited American ships from entering French and British ports.

TROUBLE IN THE NORTH

In New York and Vermont, traders ignored the embargo by using rafts to cross Lake Champlain into Canada. The smuggling led Jefferson to declare that the region was in rebellion against the government. He gave state and federal officials the power to use arms, if necessary, to end the smuggling. By the summer of 1808, troops were able to stop some of the smuggling.

The Democratic-Republicans Defend the Embargo

To Jefferson and his aides, the embargo was the best way to prevent a war with the European powers, especially Great Britain. Secretary of State James Madison believed that by denying goods to France and Britain, the two countries would work to end their war. Once the war ended, the whole issue of the United States maintaining its shipping rights as a neutral nation would also end.

Jefferson realized that the embargo would hurt some people—sailors, ship owners, merchants—but he thought that the larger goal of preventing war was worth it. The president also believed that most Americans would make personal sacrifice to show their patriotism. Some Democratic-Republicans hoped that the embargo would increase national pride. The main Democratic-Republican newspaper, the *National Intelligencer,* asserted that Americans would "flinch from no sacrifices which the honor and the good of the nation demand from virtuous and faithful citizens."

Madison and Jefferson thought that the embargo would have another positive result for the United States. Cut off from British and French goods, Americans would begin to develop their own manufacturing abilities. They already had important natural resources, such as cotton. The embargo might convince wealthy Americans to invest in factories that turned the cotton into cloth.

In general, Southerners and Democratic-Republicans across the country supported Jefferson on the embargo. They agreed with the aims of the action and were willing to make sacrifices. A South Carolinian wrote of the citizens of his state that "no people, generally speaking, bear [the embargo] more cheerfully, they are convinced it was the only prudent measure that could be pursued at the time."

> *Fast Fact*
>
> For one New Year's celebration while he was president, Jefferson ordered a new wool suit from a Connecticut wool factory to show his support for U.S. cloth manufacturing.

In Their Own Words

Here is part of a letter that Jefferson wrote in January 1808 explaining why he favored the embargo.

The embargo keeping at home our vessels, cargoes and seamen, saves us the necessity of making their capture the cause of immediate war.... Till [France and Great Britain] return to some sense of moral duty, therefore, we keep within ourselves. This gives time. Time may produce peace in Europe; peace in Europe removes all causes of difference, till another European war; and by that time our debt may be paid, our revenues clear, and our strength increased.

Attacks on the Embargo

Most of the attacks on the embargo came from the Federalists, especially in New England. They had a general hatred of Jefferson and his political ideas that went back to the 1790s. The Federalists usually favored good relations with Great Britain, and they considered Jefferson too friendly with France. Most Federalists also supported a strong national government, while Jefferson and the Democratic-Republicans usually favored keeping most power with the states.

Federalists also had specific complaints against the embargo. Many of them were involved in overseas trade and shipping or received support from voters who were so involved. The embargo had an immediate effect on the economic interests of those people. Thousands of sailors and others connected with the sea trade lost their jobs. The embargo also lowered prices for many farm goods, cutting the income of farmers. A Vermont resident described how some farmers "curse the embargo, because they cannot sell their produce and pay their debts."

Timothy Pickering, around 1800.

In Their Own Words

Senator Timothy Pickering of Massachusetts was the leading opponent of the embargo. Here is part of a letter that he wrote to New Hampshire governor James Sullivan, a Democratic-Republican. Sullivan refused to read the letter, but Pickering had it published, and thousands of copies appeared across the country.

Are our thousands of ships and vessels to rot in our harbors? Are our sixty thousand seamen and fishermen to be deprived of employment, with their families reduced to want and beggary? Are our hundreds of thousands of farmers to be compelled to suffer…[so] that our President may make an experiment on our patience and fortitude?

As Congress debated the laws that strengthened the embargo acts, the Federalist attacks grew. Some claimed that the embargo was actually part of a plan between Jefferson and Napoleon to strengthen U.S. ties with France and weaken Great Britain. The embargo was more damaging to the British, since they were America's leading trade partner. New York representative Barent Gardenier declared, "Do not go on forging chains to fasten us to the car of the Imperial Conqueror [Napoleon]."

With the Enforcement Act, parts of New England seemed ready to rebel. Some Massachusetts newspapers compared Jefferson to George III, the British king at the time of the American Revolution (1775–1783). One article said that Jefferson was a "despot who would [take]...independence from you." In Connecticut, lawmakers said that the state would not follow government laws related to the embargo that it considered unconstitutional.

The growing protests weakened some Democratic-Republicans' support for the embargo. Jefferson, however, left office convinced that the embargo could have ended Great Britain's harmful policies if it had remained in place a little longer.

> *Fast Fact*
> In 1798, Thomas Jefferson had written a document known as the Kentucky Resolutions. It claimed that states had the right to reject laws that they thought violated the Constitution. The New England states took a similar stance in opposing Jefferson and his embargo.

CHAPTER SEVEN

The War of 1812

WHAT
The issue of U.S. rights at sea causes war between the United States and Great Britain.

ISSUE
The need for war with the British

WHERE
Nationwide

WHEN
1812–1815

The roots of the War of 1812 (1812–1815) went back to the 1790s, when France and Great Britain began a series of wars that lasted until 1815. At times, the European conflict affected the United States—especially its trade with Europe and the islands of the Caribbean Sea.

In 1793, President George Washington declared that the United States would remain neutral in the wars between Great Britain, France, and their allies. Since the United States was not taking sides, it expected to be allowed to carry goods to any of the countries involved. Both the British and the French, however, sometimes stopped U.S. merchant ships bound for their enemies' ports, especially in the Caribbean. That issue, as well as several others, almost led to a war with Great Britain in 1794. Starting four years later, French and American ships fought each other on and off for several years in an undeclared naval war.

During the early 1800s, the problems at sea with France and Great Britain continued, though the United States had more difficulties with the British. One key issue was naval impressment. British sailors were often impressed—forced to serve in the navy. The British treated their sailors badly, giving them low pay and poor food. Sailors received much better treatment on American merchant ships, so many British sailors left their ships to work for the Americans. Since the 1790s, the British had sometimes stopped American ships to look for these British deserters. Claiming that some American sailors were actually British citizens, the British took them off the American ships and forced them to serve on British ships.

In 1808, President Thomas Jefferson decided to act to prevent a war with Great Britain over its practice of impressing American sailors. He called for an embargo—no U.S. ships would be allowed to leave port and trade overseas. If American ships did not sail the oceans, than British ships could not stop them and impress U.S. sailors. Jefferson also hoped that the embargo would hurt both the French and the British, since they would not receive important supplies from America. If their economies suffered enough, the two countries might consider ending their policies that hurt the United States. Perhaps they might even end their war.

> ### THE POLITICS OF THE ERA
> During Jefferson's presidency, the two major U.S. political parties were the Federalists and the Democratic-Republicans. Jefferson led the Democratic-Republicans, who generally supported France and disliked the British. Democratic-Republicans wanted the states to have as much freedom as possible to do what they chose. From 1801 through the early 1820s, the Democratic-Republicans dominated Congress and the presidency. Their opponents, the Federalists, believed in a strong national government. Many Federalists relied on shipping and foreign trade for their income. In foreign affairs, they tended to support the British and felt that Jefferson was too close to Napoleon Bonaparte, the dictator who ruled France.

The Road to War

The embargo ended up hurting the U.S. economy more than it hurt Great Britain and France. American sailors lost their jobs, and merchants and farmers did not have markets for their goods. Congress ended the embargo in March 1809 on the same day that James Madison, another Democratic-Republican, took over as president. The lawmakers replaced the embargo with a law that let U.S. ships go anywhere except to French and British ports. Trade with those countries could resume if they agreed to respect America's rights as a neutral country. Neither Great Britain nor France, however, changed its policies.

> **Fast Fact**
>
> For a brief time in 1809, President Madison thought that he had reached an agreement with Great Britain that would lead to the end of its harmful naval policies against U.S. ships. However, the British government refused to give up the right to have British sailors stop and search U.S. ships, and the deal fell through.

The British continued to be America's major concern at sea. They also seemed to be causing trouble in the western part of the United States. Native American tribes led by Tecumseh, a Shawnee chief, were protesting a sale of their land to the United States. The tribes received food and shelter from the British in Canada. When fighting broke out between U.S. troops and the Native Americans in 1811, many Americans living on the frontier accused the British of encouraging the tribes to attack. Although the British had once been allies with the Native Americans of the region, this time they had no role in the conflict between the tribes and the Americans. Still, the war fueled further American distrust of the British.

In the spring of 1812, President Madison asked Congress to declare war on Great Britain. In his message asking for war, he mentioned impressments as a major issue. He described how Americans were being "dragged on board ships of war of a foreign nation...to risk their lives in the battles of their oppressors." The president also noted that the British had not ended their policies restricting U.S. trade, and he accused them of provoking the recent war with the Native Americans.

SLOW NEWS IS NOT GOOD NEWS

Some historians suggest that the War of 1812 could have been avoided if the telegraph or another modern communication system had been in place. Two days before Congress declared war, Great Britain announced that it was ending its efforts to restrict U.S. trade. Americans, however, did not learn this for several weeks, since the news had to travel by ship across the Atlantic Ocean. Congress might not have declared war if it had known about the British action.

Famous Figures

TECUMSEH
(1768–1813)

For many years, Tecumseh fought against American settlers who moved west and tried to take over Native American lands. Joining him was his brother Tenskwatawa, who was also known as the Prophet. The Prophet told his people that they should return to their own religion and culture and not accept the white people's way of life. The Prophet's teachings helped Tecumseh recruit new warriors in a battle against the Americans. In 1811, the Prophet led a small force at Tippecanoe Creek, in present-day Indiana. U.S. troops under General William Henry Harrison—a future U.S. president—defeated the Native Americans and destroyed their village. Once the War of 1812 began, Tecumseh fought against the Americans with British aid. He died during the war, and the tribes of the region never strongly challenged the U.S. government again.

"OLD IRONSIDES"

The United States had some good news in August 1812, when the USS *Constitution* sank a British warship at sea. When a crew member saw a British cannonball bounce off the *Constitution*, he said that the wooden ship seemed as strong as iron. From then on, the ship was nicknamed "Old Ironsides." Launched in 1797, the *Constitution* was powerful and fast, and it won several other battles during the war. Today, the *Constitution*, docked in Charlestown, Massachusetts, is still considered an official U.S. Navy ship.

A Difficult War

The United States had several problems entering the war. It lacked a large army with trained officers, and its navy had just three large warships—many fewer than Great Britain's powerful naval fleet. The Americans were also split on waging a war at all. The New England states opposed the conflict, and governors there refused to send militia to help federal troops.

At the start, Madison and his aides hoped to seize Canada with several quick attacks. Instead, U.S. forces surrendered to the British at Detroit in the Michigan Territory, and an invasion of Montreal, Canada, failed. With the losses, Madison said, "the

Indians were thrown into the service of the enemy...and a general damp spread over the face of our affairs."

Many of the land battles took place near and on the Great Lakes. In January 1813, after a U.S. loss near Lake Erie, the British took about 500 prisoners, and hundreds more U.S. troops were wounded or killed. Later in the year, however, Captain Oliver Hazard Perry won a major naval battle on the lake. Other U.S. victories came in the West. At Fort Meigs, Ohio, General William Henry Harrison held off an invading British force. In October, Harrison commanded U.S. troops that defeated retreating British and Native American forces north of Lake Erie. However, the Americans faced setbacks in 1813, as well. Another invasion of Canada failed, and in June, the British captured the *Chesapeake*, one of the few U.S. warships.

In November 1813, the British told Madison that they wanted to begin peace talks. Representatives from the two sides did not meet until the following August. In the meantime, the war continued. The British struck their hardest blow over the summer, when troops landed in Maryland and marched on Washington, D.C. They set fire to the capital city, destroying the White House and many other government buildings.

President Madison knew that the country could not stay at war for long. The U.S. government was running out of money and military supplies. In addition, Great Britain had finally defeated France in Europe, so now it could focus all of its attention on the war in North America. Madison instructed the U.S. delegates at the peace talks to ignore the topic of impressment, since, with the end of the war in Europe, America's rights as a neutral were no longer an issue. Yet Madison did not want to give up too much in the peace talks. The American negotiators refused to accept the British proposal that Great Britain keep the

> *Fast Fact*
> The peace treaty that ended the War of 1812 is called the Treaty of Ghent. It is named for the city in Belgium where British and U.S. negotiators agreed to peace terms. The U.S. negotiators included John Quincy Adams, a future U.S. president.

U.S. lands that it had captured during the war. After suffering a loss in upstate New York in the fall of 1814, the British did not press this point and agreed to give back the territory that they had taken. On December 24, 1814, the two sides ended the war.

LAST BATTLE—IN PEACETIME

At the end of the war, slow communications once again played a major role. In New Orleans, Louisiana, General Andrew Jackson defeated a large, invading British force. This victory, the Battle of New Orleans, came on January 8, 1815—several weeks after British and American diplomats had signed the peace treaty. The news of the treaty did not reach the United States until February.

Supporting the War against Great Britain

Before the War of 1812 began, American opinion was split on the need to fight Great Britain. Leading the call for war were Madison and the Democratic-Republican Party. When asking Congress to declare war, the president said that the British were already in "a state of war against the United States" because of impressments and their aid to the Native Americans. The time had come, Madison said, for the states to "[oppose] force to force in defense of their national rights."

Within the Democratic-Republican Party were several young lawmakers known as War Hawks. Most came from southern and western states, and they were the strongest supporters of a war. Henry Clay, a U.S. representative from Kentucky, was one of the leading War Hawks. As early as 1810, Clay said, "I am for resistance by the *sword*."

During the next two years, more Democratic-Republicans began to agree that the British would continue to harm U.S. interests unless the United States fought for its rights. Several members of Congress wrote that the choice was between "war or submission"—fighting to end the British practices or giving up completely.

> *Fast Fact*
>
> The vote in Congress to declare war was seventy-nine to forty-nine in the House of Representatives and nineteen to thirteen in the Senate. None of the 39 Federalist members of Congress voted for war. All but 23 of the 121 Democratic-Republicans supported Madison.

Famous Figures

HENRY CLAY
(1777–1852)

Starting with the War of 1812, Henry Clay played a major role in U.S. politics for almost forty years. In 1812, he was chosen as Speaker of the House, the most important position in the U.S. House of Representatives. At the end of the war, he served as one of the negotiators in Ghent, Belgium. Clay ran for president several times, but he is best known for his work in Congress. Twice, he worked out compromises that ended harsh debates over allowing slavery in new states entering the Union. Clay also promoted what he called the American System. He wanted the national government to play a leading role in building roads and canals and helping U.S. industries grow.

The War Hawks believed that a U.S. victory would lead to American control of Canada. With Canada as part of the United States, the British would lose their base in North America—and their ability to help Native Americans who threatened U.S. settlers on the frontier. Taking Canada, some Democratic-Republicans said, was also the only way that Americans could hurt the British. Their ships dominated the seas, and the United States could not hope to use naval power to end impressments and the British restrictions on neutral trade.

Some Democratic-Republicans believed that another important issue was at stake: American honor. Since the end of the American Revolution (1775–1783), the British had not treated the United States as an equal. Great Britain seemed to think that it could use its power to mistreat the Americans. One lawmaker wrote, "It is now clearly, positively, and directly a question of...whether the [United] States are an independent nation."

In Their Own Words

Here is part of a speech by John C. Calhoun, a U.S. representative from South Carolina and a leading War Hawk.

The extent, duration, and character of the injuries received; the failure of...peaceful means...resorted to for the redress of our wrongs, is my proof that war is necessary.... The question...is reduced to this single point; which shall we do, abandon or defend our own commercial and maritime rights and the personal liberties of our citizens employed in exercising them? These rights are essentially attacked, and war is the only means of redress.

Opposing the War

To many Federalists, the War of 1812 was "Mr. Madison's War." The Federalists had always wanted good relations with the British, and they disliked Democratic-Republican attempts to confront the British. Also, the Federalist merchants of New England were still making money from their sea trade, despite the British attacks on neutral shipping. A war would hurt their economic interests. The Federalists in Congress believed that Madison had not done enough to settle problems with the British peacefully because he and the Democratic-Republicans favored the French. Others said that the United States lacked the military strength to fight and win a war.

Once the war began, some Federalists continued to oppose Madison and his policies. New England was the center of the antiwar feelings. Lawmakers in Massachusetts told the state's citizens to resist the war, and residents of Boston, Massachusetts, publicly condemned the war. Anger against the war grew so strong that some Massachusetts merchants traded with the enemy, selling supplies to the British troops stationed in Canada.

Some Federalists also saw resisting the war as a regional issue. The Democratic-Republicans were strongest in the South and West, especially in states that had entered the Union after 1790. New England was losing its power in the national government, and some lawmakers from the region felt that their concerns were not being heard in Washington. Opposing the war and refusing to aid the government was a protest against their lack of power and their belief that New England would pay more than its fair share of taxes to finance the war. The Federalists also believed that the Democratic-Republicans were more concerned about taking land—Canada—than settling the maritime issues with Great Britain. One Federalist called the conflict "a war of conquest."

> *Fast Fact*
> As Congress debated war, some Federalists wanted the United States to declare war on both Great Britain and France. They believed that the Democratic-Republicans were too pro-French. Congress rejected the idea.

The New England Federalists' anger reached its peak at the end of 1814. Delegates from the New England states met in Hartford, Connecticut, to protest the war and call for reforms in the national government. More extreme Federalists thought that the New England states should secede, or withdraw, from the Union and form their own government. The "Hartford Convention" ended just as the news of peace reached the United States.

In general, most Americans favored the War of 1812. The antiwar stance of the Federalists cost them support. In 1816, they ran their last presidential candidate, Rufus King. He won just four out of twenty states, and the Federalist Party fell apart soon after.

In Their Own Words

Here is part of a statement issued in June 1812 by Federalist congressmen who opposed the War of 1812.

What are the United States to gain by this war?... Let us not be deceived. A war of invasion may invite a retort of invasion. When we visit the peaceable, and, as to us, innocent colonies of Great Britain with the horrors of war, can we be assured that our own coast will not be visited with like horrors?

ANTIWAR DEMOCRATIC-REPUBLICANS

Not everyone who opposed the war was a Federalist. Some Democratic-Republicans shared the concern that the United States was unprepared to fight a war. Some northern Democratic-Republicans opposed the war because they disliked Madison and feared that his policies hurt the party in the North. Even some of the War Hawks were not as pro-war as they seemed. In private, many wrote letters expressing their hope that the Americans and the British could peacefully settle their differences.

CHAPTER EIGHT

The Missouri Compromise

WHAT
The United States passes laws that allow Missouri to enter
the Union as a slave state and Maine as a free state
and that limit the spread of slavery in the West.

ISSUES
*The spread of slavery into new states
and the power of Congress to limit it*

WHERE
Nationwide

WHEN
1820–1821

As early as the Constitutional Convention of 1787, some American leaders saw that slavery was a divisive issue between the states. Southern states relied on agriculture for income, and most Southerners believed that they needed African slaves to run their plantations. The North had many fewer slaves, and some states in the region were already taking steps to end slavery.

While drafting the Constitution, Northerners and Southerners had disagreed on whether or not slaves should be counted as part of a state's population. The issue was important for deciding how many representatives each state would send to the U.S. House of Representatives and how much each state would pay in taxes. Northern states had not wanted to count slaves at all for representation, but wanted to count them as full people for tax reasons. The Southern states wanted just the opposite. In the end, the delegates reached a compromise. Slaves were counted as three-fifths of a person, and the government would not address the issue of the slave trade before 1808. Each state would keep the right to decide if it would allow slavery.

For the first two decades of the nineteenth century, slavery was largely a state issue. In 1819, however, it took on national significance when the territory of Missouri applied to enter the Union as a state. Missouri had been part of the Louisiana Purchase, a large part of North America that the United States bought from France in 1803. Slavery had been legal there under French rule, and it remained legal when Missouri became a U.S. territory. Now, some Northern lawmakers wanted to place limits on slavery there as a condition for Missouri's becoming a state.

> *Fast Fact*
>
> One part of the compromise reached while writing the Constitution said that Congress could not pass laws affecting the slave trade for twenty years. In 1808, Congress finally was able to pass such a law, making it illegal to bring new slaves into the United States. An illegal slave trade, however, continued for many years.

Representative James Tallmadge Jr. of New York proposed that new slaves should not be allowed into Missouri once it became a state. He also said that any slaves born there should be freed when they turned twenty-five. Speaking for the New Yorkers that he represented, Tallmadge said, "I will proclaim their hatred to slavery in every shape." Despite complaints from Southerners, the law that the House passed allowing Missouri to enter the Union included Tallmadge's restrictions on slavery.

THE NORTHWEST ORDINANCE

Congress had considered the issue of slavery in U.S. territories once before. In 1787, a law called the Northwest Ordinance described the process for setting up governments in new lands acquired by the United States. The ordinance also spelled out how a territory could become a state. Finally, the Northwest Ordinance outlawed slavery in the Northwest Territory—the region east of the Mississippi River and north of the Ohio River. This region eventually became the states of Illinois, Ohio, Indiana, Michigan, Wisconsin, and part of Minnesota. Despite the restriction on slavery, some people illegally took slaves into the Northwest Territory.

A Need for a Compromise

When the Senate addressed the issue, another long debate began on whether or not Congress could restrict slavery in Missouri. A politician who represented Missouri in Congress noted that the topic "produced a greater sensation in Congress than was almost ever witnessed before." In the end, the Senate said that Missouri could enter the Union without any restrictions. Since the two houses of Congress could not agree, Missouri's effort to enter the Union failed.

This 1816 map shows the United States just before Missouri became a state (its southern border would be even with the boundary between Kentucky and Tennessee). Statehood for Missouri was delayed because of debates over slavery. The state was finally admitted to the Union in 1820, after approval of the Missouri Compromise.

> *Fast Fact*
>
> The state of Maine was formed out of territory that had been part of Massachusetts since the late seventeenth century.

Congress ended its work for that session soon after the Senate vote. When the new session began in December 1819, the lawmakers tried once again to settle the Missouri issue. This time, the debate had a new element. Maine, which had outlawed slavery, had applied to enter the Union. The Senate decided to link Maine and Missouri. Maine would be allowed into the Union as a free state if Missouri could enter as a slave state with no restrictions. In addition, the Senate proposed limiting the spread of slavery in the western lands purchased from France. An imaginary line drawn westward from the southern border of Missouri would mark the divide. Above the line, slavery would be outlawed; below it, a territory had the right to allow slavery.

Both Northern and Southern members of the House of Representatives resisted the Senate plan. Without a compromise, the country could split apart over the issue of slavery. As Speaker of the House, Henry Clay played the lead role in trying to get the Senate plan through the House. He proposed splitting the Senate bill into three separate parts: admitting Maine, admitting Missouri, and limiting slavery in future western states. Representatives could then vote for or against the different issues, or not vote at all, instead of accepting or rejecting the entire plan. The House then passed the three parts of "the Missouri Compromise." The closest vote came on whether or not Missouri would have restrictions on slavery. The House rejected limits by just three votes.

> *Fast Fact*
> Under the Missouri Compromise, although slavery was not allowed in the northern territories west of Missouri, escaped slaves caught in the region had to be returned to their masters.

MIXED FEELINGS ON SLAVERY

Henry Clay, from Kentucky, owned many slaves, yet he believed that slavery was harmful to both the slaves and American society. He favored a gradual end to slavery in the United States. He also thought that freed slaves should receive aid so that they could return to Africa if they chose. Years later, Clay served as president of an organization that promoted the goal of African colonization, or creating a country in Africa for freed African American slaves. These efforts led to the founding of the African nation of Liberia in 1847.

A Second Fight

At first, President James Monroe had decided he would veto, or reject, any proposal that placed limits on slavery in Missouri. He also doubted that Congress had the legal right to restrict slavery in other western territories. Still, Monroe wanted to end further arguments, so he signed the compromise even though it did have some restrictions on slavery in the territories.

> **Fast Fact**
>
> Missouri's effort to bar free blacks from the state was illegal. The Constitution says that the citizens of each state have the same rights in other states. A state cannot keep out someone who has legal rights granted by another state.

The fight to allow Missouri into the Union, however, was not over. During the summer of 1820, the residents of Missouri drafted a constitution. By law, all new states write a constitution that Congress must approve. The Missouri constitution said that free African Americans would not be allowed in the state. Angry Northern lawmakers declared that the compromise was no longer valid. The House refused to pass a resolution that granted Missouri legal status as a state.

Once again, tempers flared in Congress. One lawmaker wrote, "They begin already to talk of dissolving the Union." Members debated whether or not Missouri was actually a state, since the House had withdrawn support for its admission. Needing another compromise, Congress relied again on Henry Clay. His plan said that Congress would confirm Missouri's admission as a state if the state's legislature did not pass any law that restricted the "rights and privileges" of the citizens of other states. On a vote of eighty-seven to eighty-one, the House approved the second Missouri Compromise.

Northerners Demand Restrictions on Slavery

Some of the Northerners who opposed unlimited slavery in Missouri and the West saw the issue in moral terms. One representative who supported limits said that slavery was a "sin which sits heavy on the soul of every one of us." Average citizens also spoke out, holding meetings and issuing statements to Congress. In Philadelphia, Pennsylvania, residents said that slavery was "one of the greatest evils which exist in the United States...inconsistent with the principles upon which the independence of this nation was asserted."

To some Northern politicians, however, the issue came down to sectionalism—protecting the rights of their region. As the United States had expanded, New England and the Northeastern states had lost some of their influence to the Southern and Western states. Slave states, the Northerners argued, had an unfair advantage in the number of representatives that they had in the House. The number was based on a state's population. That total included slaves, who were counted as three-fifths of a person. As the slave population grew in Southern states, the overall population in the region—and its number of representatives—grew faster than the population in the North. New Western slave states would have this same advantage. The three-fifths count, James Tallmadge said, was only supposed to benefit the original slave-owning states—not new territories added to the Union.

If slavery were allowed to spread, the South and West would have a larger block of states with similar interests and many more representatives in Congress. If slave states controlled Congress, the North would never have a chance to limit or end slavery. Slave states could also set economic policies that favored farming, their main source of income, while hurting the commercial interests of free states.

The Northerners also argued that Congress had a constitutional right to limit slavery. Rufus King of New York noted that the original thirteen states had allowed slavery before they formed the United States. The Constitution did not specifically address either limiting it or expanding slavery. However, the Constitution gave Congress the right to pass laws regarding new territories and their entrance into the Union as states. King wrote, "Congress, may, therefore, make it a condition of the admission of a new state that slavery shall be forever prohibited within the same."

> *Fast Fact*
> At the time of the Missouri Compromise, only one U.S. president—John Adams—had come from the North. The other four had come from Virginia. Former residents of that state were also heavily involved in the politics of newer states, such as Kentucky and Tennessee.

Famous Figures

RUFUS KING
(1755–1827)

Born in Maine and educated in Massachusetts, Rufus King served as a senator from New York for twenty years. King attended the Constitutional Convention of 1787, and he supported a strong national government. He was a member of the Federalist Party, which usually promoted manufacturing and commerce over agricultural interests. King later served as the U.S. ambassador to Great Britain. In 1816, he was the last member of the Federalist Party to receive votes for president. The party dissolved after that election, though King and a few other Northeastern politicians continued to support its policies.

In Their Own Words

Here is part of a speech made by Rufus King opposing slavery in Missouri.

The existence of slavery impairs the industry and power of a nation; and it does so in proportion to the multiplication of its slaves: where the manual labor of a country is performed by slaves, labor dishonors the hands of freemen. If her laborers are slaves, Missouri may be able to pay money taxes, but will be unable to raise soldiers or to recruit seamen; and experience seems to have proved that manufacturers do not prosper where the [workers] are slaves.

The South Opposes Limits on Slavery

Southern lawmakers believed that each state had the right to allow slavery, since the Constitution did not say otherwise. The Southerners claimed that the Northerners were trying to give the national government powers that it did not have under the Constitution. President Monroe shared this view. He believed that new states had the same legal rights as the original thirteen regarding slavery.

Southerners also believed that slavery was a crucial part of their economy and way of life. They strongly resisted any Northern efforts to limit it. One Virginia representative wrote that "no incident has occurred since the adoption of this Constitution [that has produced] so much alarm with the slave-holding states." Other Virginians said that the Southern states should break apart the Union rather than give in to the North.

The Southerners saw that sectionalism was one of the issues at stake. Before Maine and Missouri applied to enter the Union, the country was evenly split between free and slave states: eleven each. If Maine entered as a free state, and if the Missouri slave restrictions passed, the balance would tip in favor of the free Northern states. Some Southerners saw the Missouri issue as the first step in a larger plan. The Northerners wanted to limit slavery throughout the West in an effort to keep Southerners out of the region. Since many Southerners owned slaves, they would be unlikely to settle in territories where slavery was outlawed. Citizens of new free states would also be more likely to elect lawmakers who would want to place further limits on slavery.

The debate over the Missouri Compromise marked the first time that slavery became a national issue in the United States. As with any compromise, the Missouri Compromise left both sides feeling that they had not gotten all they wanted. However, the arrangement kept the issue of slavery from dividing the Union—for the moment. By 1861, no compromise could prevent the North and South from battling over slavery. The result was the Civil War (1861–1865).

In Their Own Words

Here is a part of an article from a Virginia newspaper attacking the effort to limit slavery in Missouri.

When [the Northerners] have succeeded in excluding from the western settlements every Southern man, and shall have sent forth in every direction swarms from the Northern hive...a universal emancipation may be the next scheme suggested....

...Shall [Virginia] be silent when the great principles of the Constitution are assailed, when the rights of her sons, now peopling a western clime, are invaded, and principles asserted which may one day be turned with fatal effect against her own institutions?

CHAPTER NINE

Early Industry

WHAT
Business owners develop large mills that produce
cotton and other cloth.

ISSUES
The benefits of industry; the health and safety of workers

WHERE
The Northeast, particularly Massachusetts

WHEN
1820s–1840s

The first modern factories arose in England during the late eighteenth century. A number of inventors developed machines that sped up the production of textiles—cloth used to make clothing and other items. The steam engine also played a key role in creating this "Industrial Revolution." Instead of using animals or rushing rivers to power machines, factory owners used steam. The engines did not tire, as animals did, and they could be placed anywhere.

In 1790, Samuel Slater arrived in America from England. Slater had worked in one of England's cotton factories and knew how the machines worked. With help from a Rhode Island investor, he built copies of those machines and opened the first U.S. cotton mill. Americans could now take cotton grown in the South and wool from domestic sheep and turn them into textiles. The country would not have to buy these products from Britain, as it had in the past, and it could sell its textiles overseas.

SPIES IN THE FACTORY

Stealing secrets about how a company operates or makes products is called industrial espionage. Once the Industrial Revolution began in Great Britain, the government there wanted to make sure that foreigners did not steal the secrets of its textile mills. At the time, only Great Britain had these mills, so its companies could make cloth at a cheap price and control the market for it. The British government made it a crime to take overseas any textile machines or plans for building them. The U.S. government tried to avoid this law by buying machines in England, taking them apart, and shipping the parts in boxes that were supposed to be carrying other goods, such as farm tools. The British, however, were able to stop the shipments before they reached the United States. Slater relied on his memory to build textile machines similar to ones used in Great Britain.

By 1815, Rhode Island, Massachusetts, and Connecticut had more than 165 textile mills combined. Most relied on water to power the machines that turned raw cotton or wool into yarn. (Steam engines were still rare in the United States.) The mills provided thousands of jobs. Slater and other mill owners hired whole families to work in their mills, and much of the work was done by children. The owners also hired women who worked in their own homes, weaving yarn into finished cloth.

The Lowell System

For the next twenty-five years, most of the textile factories built in the United States used the methods that Slater had developed. His system was sometimes called "the Rhode Island System." In 1815, a Boston, Massachusetts, merchant drastically changed the U.S. textile industry. Francis Cabot Lowell opened a cotton mill much larger than any that Slater had designed. Lowell also put the entire manufacturing process at one site. While traveling in England a few years before, he had studied the designs of power looms, machines that wove yarn into cloth. Factories with these looms did not have to send the yarn out to local weavers, as they had in the past. Lowell built his own power loom for his mill. The entire production process was now mechanized, meaning that Lowell could produce cloth cheaper and faster than ever.

Lowell and several other investors formed the Boston Manufacturing Company. The company built its first mill in Waltham, Massachusetts. Lowell decided not to use children as workers, as Slater and English industrialists did. Instead, his company hired young, single women—most of them the daughters of local farmers. Since the Waltham factory was so large, the company also had to recruit women from other regions. Lowell built housing for the women near the factory.

In 1815 Francis Cabot Lowell introduced power looms, like those pictured in this engraving, to the United States, revolutionizing the manufacture of textiles. Most of the workers employed in Lowell's factory system were young single women, supervised by men.

The Boston Manufacturing Company's system became the new model for the U.S. textile industry. (Some smaller mills, however, lasted for several decades more.) The company soon moved to an even larger factory system, opening a series of mills in Lowell, Massachusetts. The first mill opened there in 1824, and soon more than thirty mills were operating at the site, along the Merrimack River. Across New England, new mills sprang up with new towns surrounding them. In 1826, one newspaper noted that "a busy, healthful population teems on spots over which a rabbit, a little while since, could hardly have made his way."

The Lowell factory system made a fortune for investors. It also promoted the building of public schools. Factory owners saw that they could use the schools to teach good work habits, as well as reading and writing. Students learned to follow orders, be on time, and avoid bad habits, such as drinking and gambling.

Famous Figures

FRANCIS CABOT LOWELL
(1775–1817)

Francis Cabot Lowell belonged to one of the wealthiest families in Massachusetts. He bought and sold goods overseas and had interests in banking and real estate before turning to textiles. In 1810, Lowell traveled to England and visited several textile factories, studying the power looms there. When he returned to the United States, he worked with an engineer to build a better version and then opened his first mill. Lowell died just a few years later. His business partners honored him by naming their first mill town after him.

Growth and Change

By 1850, Lowell, Massachusetts, was the second largest city in the state. In thirty years, its population had grown from 200 to 33,000. The textile industry formed the base of economic power across the North. Meanwhile, the South, using slaves to provide most of the labor, grew the cotton that the Northern mills turned into cloth. Without slavery, the North would not have had such a large supply of cheap raw material.

During this period, the Lowell workers tried several times to form unions—organizations that protected laborers from harsh working conditions and low wages. In 1834, hundreds of women "turned out"—they left their jobs to protest a pay cut. (Today, this kind of action is called a strike.) A newspaper that supported the women wrote, "The Yankee girls at Lowell are doing themselves much credit by their determined resistance of the attempt of their taskmasters to visit punishment upon them."

The textile workers also played a key role in the effort to reduce the average workday to ten hours. Most American factory workers of the 1840s worked more

Fast Fact

Massachusetts did not limit the workday to ten hours until 1874. The eight-hour day was introduced for government workers during the 1870s, but most Americans did not work eight-hour days until the 1950s.

> **Fast Fact**
>
> By 1850, Irish and French-Canadian immigrants were replacing young New England women as the main workers in the textile factories.

than twelve hours per day, six days a week. The drive for a shorter workday came as U.S. industries placed more demands on workers, pushing them to work faster.

New ideas of justice and equality developed as industries grew in the United States and Europe. Some workers began to see themselves as a distinct group. They believed that the factory owners would never willingly help them or support their interests. Textile workers continued to play a part in the growing effort to organize laborers and improve their working conditions. Real changes in the workplace, however, did not come until the twentieth century.

The Benefits of the Mills

To investors such as Francis Cabot Lowell, the textile mills were a way to make money. The machines allowed the investors' companies to produce cloth and clothing cheaper than if they used the old methods. Many U.S. politicians also saw a benefit to the new mills. Americans would use more cloth made in the United States instead of buying cloth from abroad. Money that would have left the country would instead help pay the salaries of U.S. workers. The textile companies also made money by selling their goods overseas. With their profits from domestic and foreign sales, the mill owners invested in new businesses.

To some Americans, the mills also seemed to represent progress. The country was entering a new, modern age. A few authors wrote about the huge mills in poetic terms. Harriet Farley edited a magazine for mill workers. She compared the factory to a "fairy land." A poet named John Greenleaf Whittier also praised the women who worked in the mills. In one piece, he admired their beauty and said that their jobs were noble.

The mill owners and others thought that the mills helped workers. To attract enough employees, the Lowell mills paid higher wages than most other businesses. Many of the women who dominated the workforce in Lowell welcomed the chance to leave their family's farms and earn a decent salary. Some saved their money so that they could pay for private education or help their families. Mill work made the women more independent than any earlier generation of American women. As one mill worker wrote to her sister, "The thought that I am living on no one is a happy one, indeed."

> *Fast Fact*
> Cloth manufacturers put unique symbols on their products, called trademarks. The trademarks made it easy for foreign customers to know which company had produced a certain cloth.

The town of Lowell was clean, and the women lived together in boardinghouses, paying for their rooms and meals. The food was plentiful, and the women had the chance to attend lectures and enjoy other social events together in the evenings. Housekeepers made sure that the boarders followed the company's rules against drinking alcohol, smoking, and staying out late. Visitors to Lowell and other mill towns were usually impressed by the women and their working and living conditions. In 1820, politician Henry Clay described his visit to the Boston Manufacturing Company's mill in Waltham. He said, "The greatest order, neatness, and apparent comfort reigned throughout the whole establishment."

Attacks on the Mills

Most Americans accepted the idea of manufacturing goods so that the country would not have to buy them abroad. Some people, however, believed that farming should be the main economic activity in the United States. They wanted the country to be agrarian—dominated by farms and small towns. This idea dated back to the time of the American Revolution (1775–1783). Thomas Jefferson was one of the leading supporters of the notion that farmers made good citizens who took a strong interest in their country and its government.

STRICT BUSINESS

The factories were in some ways similar to the army. Besides all the orders that workers had to follow, they had to receive a discharge before quitting their factory jobs—the same thing that soldiers receive when they leave the military. Also as in the military, the discharge could be honorable or dishonorable. A dishonorable discharge meant that a worker had been fired for breaking a company rule. A woman who received that kind of discharge could not get a job working for another textile company unless she worked under a new name.

By the time this engraving of a worker at an automated loom was made in 1844, female workers had started to speak out against the strict rules and harsh conditions of their work environments.

People who accepted this agrarian view did not want to see large factories, such as the ones that developed in Lowell. The mill owners, some critics said, were only concerned about making money, not in helping their workers or society in general. In 1823, Thomas Cooper wrote that the factories earned large sums of money for only a few investors, "at the expense of the health, life, morals, and happiness of the wretches who labor for them."

Cooper was describing the British system of manufacturing, which he assumed would be repeated in the United States. In Lowell, the first mill owners did try to improve the conditions for American workers, and in general, the U.S. factories were not as bad. Over time, however, conditions in the U.S. mills worsened. Workers and outsiders began to complain about the long hours in the factories and the strict rules that the workers had to follow both on and off the job.

In Their Own Words

In 1845, a factory worker who called herself Amelia wrote an article attacking the working and living conditions in Lowell. Here is part of what she wrote.

[A typical worker] must still continue to toil on long after Nature's lamp has ceased to lend its aid...and she must, whether she will or no, be subjected to the...inconveniences of a large crowded boarding-house where...she is obliged to sleep in a small comfortless, half ventilated apartment containing some half a dozen occupants each; but no matter...it is all well enough for her; there is no "abuse" about it; no, indeed; so think our employers—but do we think so?

In some factories, the windows were nailed shut. Warm, humid conditions kept the threads from breaking, and the temperature inside the factories often reached 90 degrees Fahrenheit (32 degrees Celsius). The workers had to bear the constant, loud noise of the machines and breathe air filled with cotton lint. Mill owners pointed out that no one forced the women to come to the mills and work long hours at a boring—and often unhealthy—job. However, Sarah Bagley, a leading labor organizer in Lowell, disagreed. "The whip that brings us to Lowell," she wrote, "is *necessity*. We must have money; a father's debts are to be paid, an aged mother to be supported.... Is this to act from free will? Is this freedom? To my mind it is slavery." The attacks on working conditions in the mills continued for decades, as workers and reformers tried to make life better for factory workers.

In Their Own Words

In 1842, British author Charles Dickens toured the United States and visited Lowell, Massachusetts. Dickens opposed industrialization, based on what he had seen in England. Life at the Lowell factories changed his mind. Here, he describes part of what he saw in Lowell.

These girls were all well dressed: and that phrase necessarily includes extreme cleanliness.... They were healthy in appearance...and had the manners...of young women: not of degraded brutes of burden.... The rooms in which they worked were as well ordered as themselves. In the windows of some, there were green plants, which were trained to shade the glass; in all, there was as much fresh air, cleanliness, and comfort, as the nature of the occupation would possibly admit to.

CHAPTER TEN

The Election of 1824

WHAT
*John Quincy Adams is elected president
by the U.S. House of Representatives.*

ISSUE
An alleged political deal made to swing the vote to Adams

WHERE
Washington, D.C.

WHEN
1825

The election of James Monroe as president in 1816 ended the first two-party political system in the United States. Monroe was a Democratic-Republican. So were the two presidents before him, James Madison and Thomas Jefferson. The Democratic-Republicans' political opponents, the Federalists, had lost popular support during and after the War of 1812 (1812–1815). By 1820, the Federalists had ceased to exist. Monroe ran for reelection without an opponent.

By 1824, however, the Democratic-Republicans were showing splits in their attitudes and policies. When the party began considering a candidate for the upcoming election, members disagreed over who it should be. That year, the traditional caucus system to choose a candidate seemed to favor one candidate, Secretary of the Treasury William Crawford.

By the spring, three other Democratic-Republicans joined Crawford as presidential candidates: Secretary of State John Quincy Adams, Representative Henry Clay of Kentucky, and Senator Andrew Jackson of Tennessee. Adams, from Massachusetts, seemed to have the least popular appeal, though he had served in Congress and was a respected diplomat. His father, John Adams, had been a devoted Federalist when he served as president from 1797 to 1801. Although the younger Adams was a Democratic-Republican, he was associated with some of the old Federalist policies and attitudes. He also lacked the personal charm and political power of Clay and the heroic past of Jackson, known as "Old Hickory," who had been a successful army general for many years. Adams admitted, "I never was and shall never be what is commonly termed a popular man."

> *Fast Fact*
>
> In 1823, William Crawford suffered a stroke, a physical ailment that affects the brain. The stroke left Crawford blind in one eye and made it difficult for him to walk. Despite his health problems, he remained in the 1824 campaign until the end.

This 1824 political cartoon shows that year's presidential election as a wild footrace run by the candidates: Andrew Jackson, John Quincy Adams, and William Crawford. In this illustration, Henry Clay has dropped out of the race.

No Clear Winner

By the fall, the candidates assumed that none of them would win enough electoral votes to become president. Under the U.S. Constitution, a candidate must win a majority of the electoral votes. These votes are awarded by special electors chosen by the states. The number of electors matches the total number of representatives that each state sends to Congress. If a candidate does not win a majority of the electoral votes, the House of Representatives elects the president, choosing from the three candidates with the most electoral votes.

During the campaign, Jackson emerged as the most popular candidate, so it was no surprise when he easily won the popular vote in the election. He also won the most electoral votes, taking 99 out of 261. Adams finished second, with 84, Crawford had 41, and Clay won 37. Since no one had a majority of the votes, Congress was to decide the election. Clay had not won enough votes to stay in the race, but he played a key role in choosing the president.

Clay was Speaker of the House, the most important position in that branch of Congress. Clay chose who served on the committees that drafted bills. In private, he sometimes worked with the committees on certain bills. Clay had the power to reward representatives who supported his aims—or punish any who opposed him. In the vote for president, Clay could convince a number of representatives to back the candidate that he wanted.

PERSONAL AND POLITICAL DISAGREEMENTS

Henry Clay had long relationships with both John Quincy Adams and Andrew Jackson. Clay and Adams had served together in Congress. They had also represented the United States in Ghent, Belgium, where the peace treaty ending the War of 1812 had been signed. At times, the two diplomats had argued over how to conduct the peace talks. Still, Clay respected Adams's intelligence and character.

Clay had harsher words for Jackson. He once called the general "ignorant...corrupt...and easily swayed by the basest men who surround him." In 1819, Clay attacked Jackson's actions in Florida, where he had captured several Spanish forts and risked starting a larger war. Jackson never forgave Clay for questioning him in public. Years later, before he died, Jackson said that one of his greatest regrets was that he hadn't shot Clay.

The House Decides

In January 1825, Clay met with Adams to discuss the upcoming House vote. Despite their past differences, the two men agreed on some issues. In Congress, Clay had worked to create what he called the American System. He pushed the national government to build roads and canals and promote manufacturing. Adams, more so than Jackson, supported the goals of the American System.

By the end of the month, the Kentucky representatives in the Houses announced that they were voting for Adams. Clay also convinced lawmakers from several other western states to back the secretary of state. Adams ended up with thirteen states—the minimum that he needed to win the election.

Immediately, Jackson's supporters complained that Clay and Adams had worked out a secret deal: Clay would support Adams and make sure that he received all or most of Clay's electoral votes. In return, Adams would name Clay the next secretary of state. In February 1825, Adams did offer Clay that position, confirming the suspicions of the Jacksonians. They said that Adams had won the presidency only by making a "corrupt bargain" with Clay.

Asserting the "Corrupt Bargain"

To Jackson and his supporters, the supposed deal between Adams and Clay was part of the tradition of corruption in Washington. Under President Monroe, the newspapers had reported several cases in which public officials tried to make money or influence events through the power that they held. The general did not think that Adams had broken any laws in the past. Even his political enemies recognized that Adams had high moral standards. However, Jackson assumed that the lure of the presidency must have clouded Adams's judgment, leading to the "corrupt bargain," and Jackson's detested rival, Clay, had obviously played a part in influencing Adams.

Once Adams had won the election, the Jacksonians erupted in anger over the supposed bargain. The Jacksonians were bitter not just because their man had lost, but because the will of the people had been denied. The greatest wrong, they felt, took place in Clay's own state. Kentucky lawmakers had passed a resolution instructing their representatives to vote for Jackson.

In the election, every Kentucky voter had chosen either Clay or Jackson—Adams had not received a single vote. However, Clay had rejected the resolution and convinced most of the other representatives to vote the way that he wanted them to vote.

Clay's accepting the job of secretary of state sealed the Jacksonians' opinion about the shady doings. Jackson compared Clay to Judas, the biblical figure who betrayed Jesus Christ for thirty pieces of silver. Jackson asked, "Was there ever witnessed such a bare faced corruption in any country before?"

Henry Clay's appointment as secretary of state after John Quincy Adams's victory in the election of 1824 confirmed for Andrew Jackson and his supporters that Clay (pictured here) and Adams had been involved in a "corrupt bargain": Clay had used his influence to convince members of Congress to vote for Adams and not Jackson.

In Their Own Words

Here is part of a letter written by Andrew Jackson Donelson, Jackson's nephew and secretary, after the election in the House.

Every corrupt act was employed to draw the Representatives from their responsibility to [the voters].... It is rumored and believed by everyone here that Mr. Clay will be made Secretary of State.... What a farce! That Mr. Adams should swear to support the constitution of the [United] States which he has purchased from Representatives who betrayed the constitution, and which he must distribute among them as rewards for the [deed].

Denying the Bargain

Neither Adams nor Clay wrote down exactly what they discussed during their long January meeting. Historians familiar with Clay and Adams do not believe that the two men made a specific trade—Clay's votes for the position of secretary of state. However, since political deals are made all the time, both probably understood what the other wanted and did not have to actually say the words. Clay could truthfully claim, as he later did, that whoever wrote the letter that appeared in the Philadelphia newspaper accusing them of making a deal was "a dastard and a liar."

Clay argued that he did not have to make a deal to support Adams—he really had no choice. Crawford was too sick to serve as president, and Jackson, he knew, would not support the American System that Clay backed.

Although the talk of a corrupt deal filled the newspapers, Adams did not say much on the subject. He saw that if he did win by a close vote, which some considered tainted, it "would open [me] to a far severer trial than defeat." Adams also said that if

> **Fast Fact**
>
> The "corrupt bargain" also haunted Clay throughout his political career. Though he served for many years in Congress, he failed in four future efforts to win the presidency.

western support helped him win the presidency, it would be natural to give a leading position to one of the region's top political figures—such as Henry Clay.

Once he won the election, Adams tried to show that he wanted the best men in his cabinet, regardless of their politics. He asked Crawford to stay on as treasury secretary, and he wanted Jackson to be his secretary of war. Both men refused. As president, Adams saw how the election of 1824 had stirred bad feelings among Jacksonians. He was never able to overcome the idea that a "corrupt bargain" had won him the presidency. Jackson focused on this issue for the next three years, and when he challenged Adams for the presidency in 1828, he easily won.

In Their Own Words

In his inaugural speech, John Quincy Adams described his hopes to overcome the divisions created by the election of 1824. Here is some of what he said.

There still remains...one sacrifice of prejudice and passion, to be made by the individuals throughout the nation who have heretofore followed the standards of political party. It is that of discarding every remnant of [hatred] against each other, of embracing as countrymen and friends....

Fellow citizens, you are acquainted with the peculiar circumstances of the recent election.... Less possessed of your confidence...than any of my predecessors, I am deeply [aware] that I shall stand more and oftener in need of your [patience].

CHAPTER ELEVEN

The Rise of the Abolitionist Movement

WHAT
A movement takes shape to abolish slavery immediately.

ISSUES
The morality of slavery; differing views on how to end slavery

WHERE
Nationwide

WHEN
1830s

Of all the issues that divided Americans during the 1800s, slavery stirred the strongest emotions. The debate over slavery led to the Civil War (1861–1865), when Southern states united to secede from the Union and form their own country, the Confederate States of America. The rise of the abolitionist movement, with its call for an immediate end to slavery, helped create the crisis between Southern slave states and the free states of the North.

When Europeans first came to North and South America, slavery was an acceptable practice with roots that were thousands of years old. The European settlers enslaved some of the Native Americans who lived in the region and then brought in slaves from Africa. Slavery filled an economic need, because colonies could not attract enough free, white workers to run the large plantations that developed in the New World. Some African slaves brought skills in trades, such as carpentry. Slavery fit in with the racist thinking of many whites. They believed that dark-skinned people, such as Native Americans and Africans, were inferior to whites. The Native Americans and Africans worshiped non-Christian gods and had different cultures. Europeans saw nothing wrong with taking Africans from their homes, denying their freedoms, and forcing them to work.

> *Fast Fact*
> Of the seven U.S. presidents who served between 1789 and 1836, five were Southerners who owned slaves.

In the United States, slavery was especially important in the South. The economy was tied to several crops raised on plantations, particularly cotton. In the North, trade and manufacturing became more important than farming, and these activities did not rely on slave labor. By 1830, all the Northern states had abolished slavery or passed laws that ended it gradually. The Southern states, however, resisted any effort to limit slavery. They also wanted slavery to be legal in new territories and states.

The Roots of the Abolitionist Movement

The first white Americans to openly oppose slavery were the Quakers, members of a religious group known as the Society of Friends. The Quakers, centered in Pennsylvania, believed that God made all humans equal and that slavery denied the equality of Africans. In 1688, one group of Quakers issued a petition that called for an end to slavery. They asked, "what thing in the world can be done worse towards us, than if men should rob or steal us away, and sell us for slaves to strange countries; separating husbands from their wives and children[?]"

During the eighteenth century, some Quakers pressured other members of the society to stop owning slaves, and in 1775, Pennsylvania Quakers started America's first antislavery organization. John Wesley, an English minister who founded the Methodist Church, also spoke out against slavery. Methodism became popular in the United States after the American Revolution (1775–1783), though American members of the church did not always condemn slavery.

Methodism spread in America as the country went through what is called the Second Great Awakening. The First Great Awakening, which began in the 1740s, was a religious movement that called for people to live by the teachings of the Bible and accept Jesus Christ as their savior. The ministers who called for this spiritual "awakening" thought that traditional ministers placed too much stress on reason and not enough on faith and emotion. The Second Great Awakening began in the 1790s and reached its peak around 1830. As during the First Great Awakening, ministers traveled across the country to give sermons and find people willing to confess their sins and accept Jesus.

> **Fast Fact**
>
> John Wesley started Methodism in 1739 while serving as a minister in the Church of England. In England, Methodism became an independent Protestant religion in 1795. An American form of Methodism began in 1784.

The Second Great Awakening helped many Americans find a deeper faith in Christianity. The ministers who led it also called on people to act on their faith. Good Christians, the ministers said, should try to improve society and oppose harmful practices—such as slavery. The ideas of the Second Great Awakening influenced some of the abolitionists who emerged after 1830.

Other abolitionists agreed with the writings of David Walker, who in 1829 published *An Appeal to the Colored People of the World*. Walker, a free black, saw that the American ideas of liberty conflicted with slavery. Walker also attacked a popular idea of the day—that free blacks should be sent back to Africa, a process called colonization. "Tell us no more about colonization," he wrote, "for America is as much our country, as it is yours."

Famous Figures

DAVID WALKER
(1785–1830)

Although white writers and speakers dominated the early abolitionist movement, free blacks also played a role. One of the most important was David Walker. The son of a free black woman and slave father, Walker had grown up free in North Carolina. During the 1820s, he settled in Boston, Massachusetts, where he began speaking against slavery and for the rights of blacks. His *Appeal* called for slave rebellions, which frightened many Southerners. State officials tried to keep the pamphlet out of the South, and in some states, toughened laws that forbade teaching slaves how to read.

Garrison and *The Liberator*

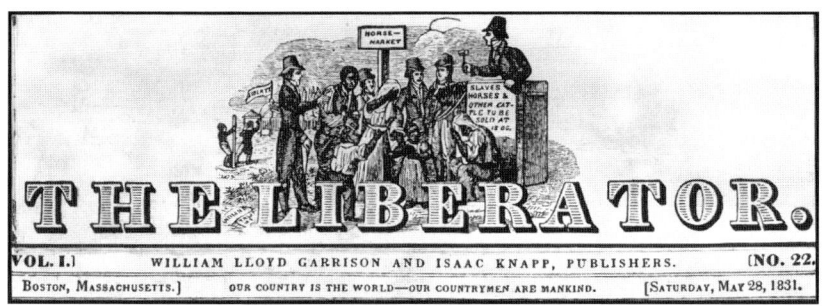

The masthead of William Lloyd Garrison's The Liberator, *from May 28, 1831.*

The abolitionist movement gathered steam in 1831 when William Lloyd Garrison introduced *The Liberator*. In this newspaper, Garrison called for an immediate end to slavery throughout the United States. In his first issue, Garrison insisted that he would be "as harsh as truth, and as uncompromising as justice" in his effort to end slavery. People who agreed with Garrison's firm call for immediate abolition were sometimes called Garrisonians. During the 1830s, these people included Wendell Phillips, a Massachusetts lawyer, author Lydia Maria Childs, also from Massachusetts, and Angelina Grimké Weld and Sarah Grimké, two sisters from South Carolina.

In 1833, Garrison helped found the American Anti-Slavery Society (AASS). Its members traveled through the North, speaking against slavery. The abolitionists faced physical dangers as they spread their message. A mob once threatened to kill Garrison, and in 1837, an abolitionist newspaper editor in Illinois was killed for his views.

Over time, the AASS split apart, because some members thought that the strict Garrisonians should be more flexible. Some abolitionist ministers, for example, were not comfortable keeping slave owners out of their churches, as the Garrisonians demanded. Garrison and his followers also believed that women should have equal rights with men, including, for example, the right to speak publicly at antislavery meetings. Most Americans of the 1830s rejected this notion.

The abolitionist movement also led to divisions within some religions. During the 1840s, both the Methodists and Baptists split into separate camps along geographic lines. Southern members of these churches did not openly oppose slavery, while the Northerners saw it as a sin. Still, many Northern Methodists and Baptists did not call for immediate abolition, as the Garrisonians did. Those who did sometimes formed their own smaller religious groups.

Famous Figures

WILLIAM LLOYD GARRISON
(1805–1879)

William Lloyd Garrison was America's first major abolitionist. Trained as a printer in Boston, Garrison was influenced by Benjamin Lundy, a Quaker writer who actively opposed slavery. Garrison's religious beliefs were also shaped by the ideas of the Second Great Awakening. He spent time in Baltimore, Maryland, before returning to Boston and starting his antislavery newspaper. He considered the U.S. Constitution a proslavery document and said abolitionists should not support the government as long as it tolerated slavery. Although best known as an abolitionist, Garrison also opposed war and supported equal rights for free blacks.

Despite the splits and arguments, the most faithful abolitionists continued to voice their views against slavery. In politics, however, they could not gain influence. Even people who opposed slavery thought that the leading abolitionists were too extreme. Most Northern politicians wanted to stop the spread of slavery and then gradually end it. Most Southerners still supported slavery and hated the abolitionists.

The Arguments for Abolitionism

Most abolitionists based their beliefs on the Declaration of Independence and the Bible. In the Declaration, Thomas Jefferson wrote, "All men are created equal." Garrison accepted this idea completely—even as he acknowledged that the Declaration was written by a man who owned slaves and that the signers of the Declaration also accepted slavery. Those men, like all people, made mistakes. Their view of slavery was a mistake.

Religion was a key part of the abolitionist movement. Slavery, to many Northerners, was a sin. Opposing slavery in general, yet still accepting its existence, was wrong. Garrison had once called for the gradual end of slavery, but in his first edition of *The Liberator*, he "[asked] pardon of my God...for having uttered a statement so full of...injustice and absurdity."

Some abolitionists turned to specific parts of the Bible to explain their beliefs. They noted a line from the book of Exodus, part of the Old Testament: "He that stealeth a man, and selleth him, shall be put to death." Africans were stolen from their homes and then sold into slavery. Even if slave owners did not actually do the stealing and selling, they took part in the process. Southerners also sold slaves born on their plantations. They were involved in an evil system condemned by God.

That system, the abolitionists said, damaged all Americans. The slaves themselves obviously suffered. They had no freedom, they could not go to school, and they were often tortured. The masters were destroying their relationship with God by owning slaves. James Freeman Clarke, an antislavery minister, believed that "society is poisoned in its roots by the system."

This depiction of a slave market was an original drawing made for the 1832 book Uncle Tom's Cabin *by Harriet Beecher Stowe.*

In Their Own Words

Theodore Weld was a well-known abolitionist minister of the 1830s and 1840s. Here is a selection from his 1839 book, *American Slavery As It Is*.

...Slaveholders talk of treating men well, and yet not only rob [slaves] of all they get...but rob them of themselves also...their bodies and their minds, their time and liberty and earnings, their free speech and rights of conscience, their right to acquire knowledge and property and reputation.

Opposition to Abolitionism

The strongest opponents of the abolitionist movement were slave owners and people who supported the right of others to own slaves. Most were Southerners, though a few Northerners also accepted allowing slavery in the United States. Many Northerners also had racist views of blacks. Like the abolitionists, the supporters of slavery often turned to the Bible to argue their point.

Proslavery ministers cited Ham, the son of Noah. In the book of Genesis, Noah curses Ham's son Canaan, saying he will have to serve as a slave. Other relatives of Ham were dark-skinned. Southerners concluded that Africans were descendants of Ham and had inherited the curse put on Canaan. Other defenders of slavery noted that slavery existed in biblical times. Saint Paul wrote that slaves should obey their masters, and he once told an escaped slave to return to his master.

Some slave owners insisted that slavery was actually good for the slaves. They said that slaves lacked the intelligence and political skills to care for themselves in

> *Fast Fact*
> In 1852, Harriet Beecher Stowe published *Uncle Tom's Cabin,* the strongest antislavery book written in America. Stowe used Weld's *American Slavery As It Is* for reference while writing her book.

> **Fast Fact**
>
> Some Northern churches supported the American Colonization Society, the main group seeking to send free blacks back to Africa.

a free society such as the United States, so slavery was, in the words of one Southern lawmaker, "a positive good." American slaves, others argued, lived better than slaves in Africa or poor people in Europe.

Abolitionists also faced opposition from "gradualists"—people who opposed slavery but did not think that the country could end it immediately. This group included some Southern slave owners, such as Senator Henry Clay. Other gradualists were Northerners who believed that slavery was wrong but thought that the abolitionists' ideas and practices would create social disorder. William Ellery Channing, a famous Boston minister, said that he honored abolitionists "for their strength of principle," but thought that they were "unfriendly to the spirit of Christianity" because they called slave owners "monsters of cruelty and crime."

The abolitionist movement of the 1830s and 1840s was never large. Too many Americans feared its methods and attitudes. However, the abolitionists forced the country to confront America's "peculiar institution," the enslavement of African Americans.

In Their Own Words

Here is part of an 1835 speech by George McDuffie, governor of South Carolina.

No human institution, in my opinion, is more...consistent with the will of God than domestic slavery.... Whether we consult the [Bible] or the lights of nature and reason, we shall find these truths as abundantly apparent as if written with a sunbeam in the heavens.... In all respects, the comforts of our slaves are greatly superior to those of the English...to say nothing of the millions of paupers crowded together in those loathsome...public poorhouses.

CHAPTER TWELVE
The Nullification Crisis

WHAT
South Carolina attempts to nullify a tariff.

ISSUE
The ability of a state to ignore or overturn a federal law

WHERE
South Carolina

WHEN
1832–1833

After the War of 1812 (1812–1815), manufacturing began playing a larger role in the U.S. economy. Mills produced wool and other cloth, while factories turned out clocks and tools. Some Americans called on the U.S. government to promote new industries so that the country would not need to buy goods abroad. New industries also meant jobs for workers and wealth for the people who invested in manufacturing companies. Other companies made money providing raw materials for the factories. The policies designed to boost industry in the United States were known as the American System.

The American System included tariffs, which are taxes placed on foreign goods entering the country. A tariff raises the prices of foreign goods, making people less likely to buy them if American-made products are available at a lower price. Tariffs also let U.S. manufacturers charge more for their products than they might normally, as long as their price is still below the cost of the foreign product.

In 1828, Congress passed a bill that placed a tariff on foreign wool, iron, molasses, and liquor. Lawmakers from states that produced the taxed items or that made finished products out of them supported the tariff, since it would increase the sales of their own goods. In the South, however, people protested the tariff. The Southern states relied on farming, not manufacturing, for income. The tariff meant that they would have to pay more for many common goods, while still receiving the same income for the crops that they produced.

Vice President John C. Calhoun emerged as one of the leading opponents of the tariff. He secretly wrote a

> *Fast Fact*
>
> Henry Clay, a Kentucky lawmaker, was the best-known supporter of the American System. Clay and his political allies were sometimes called nationalists. They sought economic policies that strengthened the national government, as opposed to keeping most power with the states.

paper attacking the tariff, declaring that a state had the right to nullify, or overturn, a national law that was unconstitutional. Calhoun's ideas were used in his native South Carolina to signal that state's opposition to the tariff. South Carolina's government asserted that if the tariff were enforced, the "the fate of this fertile state would be poverty and utter desolation." To some Southerners, the tariff was an "abomination."

Famous Figures

JOHN C. CALHOUN
(1782–1850)

The son of a South Carolina politician, John C. Calhoun served as secretary of war under James Monroe and was twice elected vice president. He is perhaps best known for his service in Congress, where he sat for more than twenty years. In 1812, as members of the House of Representatives, Calhoun and Henry Clay were two of the leading War Hawks, lawmakers eager to fight Great Britain. During his years in the Senate from 1832 to 1850, Calhoun defended slavery and sought to protect states' rights. He believed that his political opponents illegally tried to expand the powers of the national government at the expense of the states.

A contrast between two merchants is shown in this 1832 political cartoon. The merchant on the right, under regular government taxes, is prosperous. The merchant on the left, suffering under the tariffs imposed in 1828 and 1832, has shut down his business.

The Tariff of 1832

Despite the protests in South Carolina, the tariff of 1828 remained in place. Four years later, Congress considered a new tariff law. Henry Clay wanted the highest tariffs that he could get because they promoted the American System. Southerners wanted deep reductions in the tariffs, if they could not be repealed altogether. President Andrew Jackson favored a middle course—reducing the tariffs, but not as much as the Southerners wanted.

A congressional committee led by John Quincy Adams, a former U.S. president, worked out a compromise. The tariff was eliminated on a few products and reduced on others, but the tax rate remained high on such common items as wool and cotton products and iron. Jackson accepted the new tariff, but South Carolinians did not.

Since 1828, some political leaders in South Carolina had continued to talk about nullification. The new tariff law further stirred their anger. Crowds gathered in the city of Charleston to protest the tariff. In Washington, Jackson heard rumors that the nullifiers were trying to convince U.S. military officers to support their cause. The president didn't think that the nullifiers had the "madness and folly" to carry out a rebellion. Still, he had to be prepared if they took drastic action. He put U.S. troops in Charleston on alert and replaced any officers he thought might support the nullifiers.

Meanwhile, South Carolina's lawmakers continued to pursue nullification. In November 1832, the state legislature declared that the tariffs of both 1828 and 1832 were "null, void, and no law." The lawmakers also said that starting the next February, it would be illegal to collect the tariff within the state's borders. If the U.S. government tried to use force against the state, South Carolina was prepared to secede, or leave the Union and form its own country.

Jackson was not prepared to allow South Carolina to nullify the tariffs or secede. He said that South Carolinians would be committing treason if they defied the government and tried to secede. He wrote, "The union must be preserved."

Across the country, most Americans welcomed Jackson's public statements against nullification and South Carolina's threat to leave the Union. Still, the nullifiers were not ready to give in, and many South Carolinians prepared for a battle. So did Jackson. He outlined to Congress what he would do if violence broke out in South Carolina. With a few congressional changes to existing laws, he would have the authority to call in troops. Jackson's proposal for possible military action was called the Force Bill. To his critics, it was "the War Bill" or "the Bloody Bill."

> *Fast Fact*
> Tariffs were sometimes called protectionist measures—they protected American manufacturers from larger and wealthier foreign competitors. The foreign competition often had better production methods and therefore could make and sell goods at lower prices. Tariffs were also the main source of money for the government, since the United States did not have an income tax at that time.

TROUBLE IN GEORGIA

While wrestling with South Carolina and the tariff issue, President Jackson also faced difficulties with Georgia. In 1830, Jackson had called for a government policy of "Indian removal"—forcing Native American tribes off their traditional lands and moving them west of the Mississippi River. Jackson hoped that the Cherokee and other tribes in the Southeast would leave peacefully, but they resisted. Georgia, in the meantime, was trying to take control of Cherokee lands. The Cherokee and their white supporters challenged a law that limited contacts between whites and Native Americans. In 1832, the U.S. Supreme Court overturned the law, but Georgia refused to follow the court's ruling. Jackson did not take any action against Georgia, since he wanted the Cherokee to leave the state. He also did not want to upset Georgia's leaders and have them join with South Carolina on the nullification issue.

Ending the Crisis

Before Congress voted on Jackson's plans for military action, the president tried to find a peaceful solution to the nullification crisis. Jackson and his aides drafted a new tariff law. It called for large cuts on the tariffs for most items covered in the 1828 and 1832 laws. The proposed changes, Jackson hoped, would ease concerns in South Carolina. Manufacturers, however, were upset with the effort to limit protectionism.

At this point, Henry Clay stepped into the debate. He hoped to prevent war with South Carolina and give the manufacturers as high a tariff as possible. He called for keeping the tariffs until 1842, then cutting them drastically. The delay in cuts would give manufacturers more time to improve their methods, reduce their costs, and compete with foreign companies. In return, South

Fast Fact

On February 20, 1830 the Force Bill passed in the Senate by a vote of thirty-two to one. Senators who favored nullification walked out of the Senate without voting on the bill. The one negative vote came from John Tyler—a future U.S. president.

Carolina would see the tariffs eventually end—and the country would avoid conflict. "I wish to see war of no kind," Clay told the Senate, "but, above all, I do not desire to see civil war."

John C. Calhoun supported Clay's proposal, but Congress still hotly debated the plan's details. Finally, on February 26, the House approved the plan, and the Senate followed three days later. On March 4, Jackson signed the Compromise Tariff and the Force Bill—but he would not need to use force in South Carolina. The nullification threat was over.

The Argument for Nullification

Calhoun and other South Carolina politicians saw the 1828 tariff as an attack on the Constitution. In their minds, Congress had the right to collect a tariff if the goal was to provide money for the government. However, the Constitution did not say that Congress could promote the interests of one group of people—manufacturers—over the interests of others. Since Congress was not granted that right, only the states had the right to protect manufacturing.

The nullifiers also argued that the Constitution did not prevent the states from nullifying a national law. The Supreme Court had taken on the power of deciding if a law was constitutional, but the Constitution itself did not grant the court that power. Calhoun and the nullifiers argued that a state also had the legal right to reject an unconstitutional law. The power of government, or sovereignty, rested in the people. The people, through their representatives, had written and approved the Constitution. Now, the sovereign people could reject laws that went beyond the powers that they had given to the national government in the Constitution. The tariff, with its unfair promotion of manufacturing, went beyond those granted powers.

By 1832, the South Carolinians were turning to the past to find support for their position. In 1798, Thomas Jefferson had denounced the Alien and Sedition Acts. These laws had restricted

> *Fast Fact*
>
> In 1798, James Madison also wrote against the legality of the Alien and Sedition Acts. His ideas were used in the Virginia Resolutions, which South Carolinians also used to support their arguments for nullification.

free speech and the rights of immigrants. Kentucky used Jefferson's words when it passed resolutions attacking the laws. The Kentucky Resolutions argued that states could reject unconstitutional laws, and Kentucky's leaders judged that the Alien and Sedition Acts were unconstitutional. A second set of resolutions, from 1799, specifically used the term "nullification." The 1799 resolutions also seemed to support a state's right to secede over a constitutional issue. Given Jefferson's position as the writer of the Declaration of Independence and a former president, the South Carolina nullifiers considered his ideas influential.

By the end of 1832, the nullifiers controlled South Carolina's government, and they spoke openly of war and secession. Governor Robert Hayne, speaking for the antitariff leaders, said, "we will stand or fall with Carolina." Some other Southern states supported South Carolina's attack on the tariff, but not its views on nullification. Alabama's lawmakers said that nullification was "unsound in theory and dangerous in practice." South Carolinians also saw that Jackson was serious about preserving the Union and the government's right to collect the tariff. With the Compromise Tariff of 1833, the nullifiers lost influence in South Carolina.

A CONCERN ABOUT SLAVERY

For many nullifiers, the tariff issue went beyond the taxing of foreign goods. They feared that the tariff could lead to future attacks on slavery. The tariff and the move to stop nullification seemed to threaten the states' power. If Congress was allowed to go ahead with the tariff, it might take future steps that limited the states' freedom—such as ending their right to allow slavery.

In Their Own Words

Here is part of the "South Carolina Exposition and Protest of 1828," calling for nullification of the tariff.

The representatives of [South Carolina], anxiously desiring to live in peace with their fellow citizens, and to do all that in them lies to preserve and perpetuate the union of the states and liberties...but feeling it to be their...duty to expose and resist all [threats] upon the true spirit of the Constitution...claim to enter upon the journal of the Senate their protest against [the tariff] as unconstitutional, oppressive, and unjust.

The Attack on the Nullifiers

Both supporters and opponents of the tariff spoke out against the nullifiers. As president, John Quincy Adams had supported the American System. In 1831, he criticized Calhoun and the nullification effort. A state that ignored a national law was rebelling, not asserting a constitutional right.

Another critic was James Madison, the main author of the U.S. Constitution. He thought that the South Carolinians misread the Constitution and his writings in 1798 on the Alien and Sedition Acts. Madison said that the country would face chaos if each individual state could interpret—or reject—a national law for its own benefit. Differences in how state officials and the national government defined or carried out laws could lead to "collisions incompatible with the peace of society and with that regular and efficient administration which is of the essence of free governments."

President Jackson was left to find a way to end the nullification crisis. Never a fan of protectionism, he was willing to cut the tariffs immediately. When he saw that he did not have enough votes in Congress to do that, he accepted Clay's Compromise Tariff. He also spoke strongly against a state's supposed right to nullify a law or secede from the Union. Jackson had not been considered a nationalist before the tariff issue arose. He usually supported states' rights. In this case, however, he saw the need to preserve the Union and defend the Constitution. The United States, he believed, had been formed by the people, not by state governments. A state government could not deny the will of all the people, as expressed in Congress. A state also could not break apart the Union formed by individuals in all the states. No state had the right to secede—an argument Abraham Lincoln repeated almost thirty years later, at the start of the Civil War (1861–1865).

In Their Own Words

Here is part of a message that Andrew Jackson delivered on December 10, 1832, to the people of South Carolina, attacking their positions on nullification and secession.

I consider, then, the power to annul a law of the United States, assumed by one state, incompatible with the existence of the Union, contradicted expressly by the letter of the Constitution, unauthorized by its spirit, inconsistent with every principle on which it was founded, and destructive of the great object for which it was formed....

Our Constitution does not contain the absurdity of giving power to make laws and another to resist them.... the states, when they... ratified it, [did not] do so under the impression that a veto on the laws of the United States was reserved to them.

Glossary

allies—friends and supporters of a person or country

ambassador—a person who represents a government in a foreign country

amendment—a change or addition to a legal document

annul—to legally overturn a law or its effects

bill—a proposal for a new law

blockade—a military effort to prevent goods or ships from entering or leaving a country

cabinet—a group of advisers to a leader

cede—to give up the legal right to claim territory

civil—relating to a government, its citizens, and their affairs

conspiracy—a plot among a group of people to carry out an illegal action

corruption—the use of illegal methods to gain money or power

delegate—a person chosen to represent others at a meeting or convention

despotism—a government system with one powerful ruler who denies citizens their freedom

domestic—relating to issues or products within a country's borders

embargo—a legal effort to prevent goods from entering or leaving a country

emperor—a person with complete power over a country and the other lands that it controls

expedition—a trip to explore an unknown area

factions—groups with opposing political views

inauguration—the ceremony giving an elected presidential candidate the powers of the office

legislature—the part of a government that makes laws

maritime—relating to the sea

mechanized—done by machinery

militia—a part-time military force composed of local citizen volunteers

moral—correct, as defined by religious or legal teachings

naturalization—the process that makes an immigrant to a nation a legal citizen

oppressors—people who deny the legal rights of others

ordinance—a law passed by local officials

petition—a request to the government to carry out some action, or the actual document making that request

plantations—large farms where usually just one crop is grown for sale

radical—extreme in thoughts or actions, compared to most members of a community

ratify—to formally approve a suggested action

redress—payment or action to make up for a harmful act

repeal—to overturn a law

resolution—a statement of belief or desire to take action

secede—to formally withdraw from a political organization

sovereignty—the authority to govern

testimony—statements made during a court case

treason—any attempt to overthrow or weaken a legal government

Bibliography

BOOKS

Behrman, Carol H. *Andrew Jackson*. Minneapolis: Lerner Publications, 2003.

Blumberg, Rhoda. *What's the Deal? Jefferson, Napoleon, and the Louisiana Purchase*. Washington, DC: National Geographic Society, 1998.

Collier, Christopher, and James Lincoln Collier. *The Jeffersonian Republicans, 1800–1823*. New York: Benchmark Books, 1999.

Hakim, Joy. *A History of US: The New Nation*. 3rd ed. New York: Oxford University Press, 2003.

Peterson, Helen Stone. *Henry Clay: Leader in Congress*. New York: Chelsea House, 1991.

Volo, James M., and Dorothy Denneen Volo. *Encyclopedia of the Antebellum South*. Westport, CT: Greenwood Press, 2000.

Weber, Michael. *The Young Republic*. Austin: Raintree Steck-Vaughn, 2000.

Whitelaw, Nancy. *Thomas Jefferson: Philosopher and President*. Greensboro, NC: Morgan Reynolds, 2002.

WEB SITES

African American Mosaic—Influence of Prominent Abolitionists
lcweb.loc.gov/exhibits/african/afam006.html

Digital History—Guided Readings: The Era of Good Feelings
www.digitalhistory.uh.edu/database/subtitles.cfm?titleID=81

Digital History—Guided Readings: Jacksonian Democracy
www.digitalhistory.uh.edu/database/subtitles.cfm?titleID=92

HistoryCentral.com—War of 1812
www.multied.com/1812/Index.html

National Humanities Center Online Professional Development Seminar Toolboxes—The Triumph of Nationalism/The House Dividing: Nationalism and Sectionalism in the United States: 1815–1850
www.nhc.rtp.nc.us/pds/triumphnationalism/triumphnationalism.htm71

Cumulative Index

A

AAPA. *See* Association Against the Prohibition Amendment
AASS. *See* American Anti-Slavery Society
abolitionists
   Vol. 2: 114–122
   Vol. 3: 62–63, 89, 102, 103
   Vol. 4: 110
abortion
   Vol. 1: 9
   Vol. 2: 9
   Vol. 3: 9
   Vol. 4: 9
   Vol. 5: 8, 9, 62, 62–74, 66, 68, *70, 73*, 85
absentee ballot, Vol. 5: 125
Adams, Abigail
   Vol. 1: 100, *100*
   Vol. 3: 52
Adams, John
   Vol. 1: 75, 87, 94, 95, 96, 98
   Vol. 2: *33*, 33–34
Adams, John Quincy
   Vol. 2: 106, 108–112
   Vol. 3: 109
Adams, Samuel, Vol. 1: 83, 87–88, 89
Addams, Jane, Vol. 4: 88
affirmative action, Vol. 5: 100–110, *101, 103, 104, 107*
African Americans
   Vol. 3:
      Andrew Johnson and, 123, 124
      civil rights for, *112*, 112–120, *116*
      freeing of the slaves, 102–110, *105, 108*
      secession of Southern states and, *92*, 92–100, *94, 97*
   Vol. 4:
      election of 1876 and, 13, 14, 17, 19
      Plessy v. Ferguson, *52*, 52–58, *54*
      Republican policy toward, 12
      in suffragist movement, 112
   Vol. 5:
      affirmative action and, 100, 102, 107–108, 109, 110
      Brown v. Board of Education, 36–46, *38, 44*
      election of 2000 and, 129
      Vietnam War and, 59
Agricultural Adjustment Administration, Vol. 4: 126
Aguinaldo, Emilio, Vol. 4: 68
alcohol, Vol. 4: 100–108, *101, 106*

Alexander, James, Vol. 1: 53
Alien and Sedition Acts,
   Vol. 2: 24–30Alien Enemies Act, Vol. 2: 24–25, 28–29
alimony, Vol. 5: 84
Allen, John, Vol. 2: 29
Allies
   Vol. 1: 133
   Vol. 5: 133. *See also* Triple Entente
Almond, Lincoln, Vol. 5: *123*
Altgeld, John Peter, Vol. 4: 47, 49
AMA. *See* American Medical Association
Amalgamated Society of Engineers, Vol. 4: 46
ambassador, Vol. 5: 133
Amelia (factory worker), Vol. 2: 103
amendment
   Vol. 1: 128, 133
   Vol. 5: 133. *See also* specific amendments
American Anti-Slavery Society (AASS), Vol. 2: 117 Vol. 3: 53
An American Dilemma (Myrdal), Vol. 5: 43
American Liberty League, Vol. 4: 130
American Medical Association (AMA), Vol. 5: 64
American Revolution, Vol. 1: 80–90, *84, 86*
American Slavery As It Is (Weld), Vol. 2: 121
American System
   Vol. 2: 124
   Vol. 4: 73
American Woman Suffrage Association (AWSA), Vol. 4: 110, 112
amicus curiae briefs, Vol. 5: 106, 107
ammunition, Vol. 1: 133
anarchists, Vol. 4: 43, 44–50
Anglicanism, Vol. 1: 60
annexation of Texas, Vol. 3: 32–40
Anthony, Susan B.
   Vol. 3: 119
   Vol. 4: 110, 111
anti-communism, Vol. 5: 24–34, *27, 28, 30*
anti-Federalists, Vol. 1: 125–132
Anti-Saloon League (ASL), Vol. 4: 101, 102–103, 105
anti-suffrage movement, Vol. 4: 118–120
Antis, Vol. 4: 118–120
antiwar movement, Vol. 5: *51*, 51, 57–60, 59
An Appeal to the Colored People of the World (Walker), Vol. 2: 116

armory
   Vol. 3: 133
   Vol. 4: 133
Articles of Confederation, Vol. 1: 104–112, *108*, 114–122
ASL. *See* Anti-Saloon League
assembly centers, Vol. 5: 14–15
assembly lines, Vol. 4: 72
Association Against the Prohibition Amendment (AAPA), Vol. 4: 107, 108
Association for the Study of Abortion, Vol. 5: 65
atomic bomb, Vol. 5: 26, 29
atonement, Vol. 1: 133
Austin, Stephen, Vol. 3: 32
Austria-Hungary, Vol. 4: 80
automobile industry, Vol. 4: *70*, 70–78, *71, 76*
AWSA. *See* American Woman Suffrage Association

B

B & O. *See* Baltimore and Ohio Railroad
Bacon, Nathaniel, Vol. 1: 33–40, *35, 36*
Bacon's Rebellion, Vol. 1: 32–40, *35, 36*
Baker, Newton D., Vol. 4: 130
Bakke, Allan, Vol. 5: *101*, 101–103, 103
Ball, George, Vol. 5: 59
ballot, Vol. 5: 124–132, *128*, 133
Baltimore and Ohio Railroad (B & O), Vol. 4: 24–25, 28
Bank of the United States (BUS), Vol. 3: 22–30, *23*
Bank War. *See* Bank of the United States
Baptist church, Vol. 1: 15, 64–65, 67
Battle of Buena Vista, Vol. 3: *45*
Beecher, Henry Ward, Vol. 4: 29
Bell, John, Vol. 3: 94, *94*
Bennett, William, Vol. 5: 119
Bentley, Elizabeth, Vol. 5: 28
Benton, Thomas Hart, Vol. 3: 24
Berkeley, William, Vol. 1: 32–40
Berle, Adolf, Jr., Vol. 4: 128
Beveridge, Albert, Vol. 4: 66
Bible, Vol. 4: 118–119
Biddle, Francis, Vol. 5: 20–21
Biddle, Nicholas, Vol. 3: 24, 25
Bill of Rights, Vol. 1: 125, 128
Bingham, John A., Vol. 3: 117
Bishop, Bridget, Vol. 1: 45
Black Codes
   Vol. 3: 113, 114, 117
   Vol. 4: 52–53
   Vol. 5: 42
Black Hawk, Vol. 3: 16
Black, Hugo, Vol. 5: 19
Blackmun, Harry, Vol. 5: 67, 71
Blackstone, William, Vol. 3: 60

"Black Thursday," Vol. 4: 124
Blatch, Harriet Stanton, Vol. 4: 113
blockades, Vol. 2: 64–65
Bok, Derek, Vol. 5: 106–107
Boland Amendment, Vol. 5: 90–91
Boland, Edward, Vol. 5: 91
Boland II, Vol. 5: 91, 95
Bollinger, Lee, Vol. 5: 104
Bolton, John, Vol. 5: *128*
Bonaparte, Napoleon, Vol. 2: 44, 45
bootlegging, Vol. 4: 104, 108
Borah, William, Vol. 4: 95
Border Ruffians, Vol. 3: 75
Boston (MA), Vol. 1: 80–83
Boston Manufacturing Company, Vol. 2: 97–98
Boston Massacre, Vol. 1: 80
Boston Tea Party, Vol. 1: 80, 81
Boutwell, George, Vol. 3: 128
Bradford, William, Vol. 1: 17, 53, 55
Bradley, Joseph, Vol. 4: *18*, 18, 53
Bradley, Richard, Vol. 1: 54, 55, 56
Brain Trust, Vol. 4: 128
Brattle, Thomas, Vol. 1: 49–50
Breckenridge, John, Vol. 3: 93, 94, *94*
Brennan, William
    Vol. 1: 9
    Vol. 2: 9
    Vol. 3: 9
    Vol. 4: 9
    Vol. 5: 9
Briggs, Harry, Vol. 5: 38, 44
Briggs v. Elliot, Vol. 5: 38–39, 42
Brown, Henry Billings, Vol. 4: 58
Brown, John, Vol. 3: 76
Brown, Linda, Vol. 5: 39, *44*
Brown v. Board of Education, Vol. 5: 38, 39–46, *44*, 67, 100
Buchanan, James, Vol. 3: 88, 99
Bumpers, Dale, Vol. 5: 120
Burke, Edmund, Vol. 1: 90
Burke, Thomas, Vol. 1: 112
Burlingame, Anson, Vol. 4: 34
Burlingame Treaty, Vol. 4: 34
Burr, Aaron, Vol. 2: 37, 52–62, *61*
Burr Conspiracy, Vol. 2: 52–62
Burton, Charles, Vol. 5: *128*
BUS. *See* Bank of the United States
Bush, George H.W.
    Vol. 5:
        affirmative action and, 105
        defeat by Bill Clinton, 112
        George W. Bush and, 122
        internment of Japanese Americans and, 18
        Iran-Contra affair and, 94, 95
Bush, George W.
    Vol. 4: 20
    Vol. 5: 122–132
Bush, Jeb, Vol. 5: 122
Bush v. Gore, Vol. 5: 130
butterfly ballot, Vol. 5: 128, 129, 131

C

cabinet
    Vol. 3: 133
    Vol. 4: 133
    Vol. 5: 133
Calef, Robert, Vol. 1: 50
Calhoun, John C.
    Vol. 2: 82, 124–125, *125*, 129
    Vol. 3: 37–38, 48, 67–69
California
    Vol. 3: 63, 64
    Vol. 4: 32–40, *33*, *37*, *38*
    Vol. 5: 12, 109
Calvinists, Vol. 1: 12–20
Calvin, John, Vol. 1: 12
Cambodia, Vol. 5: 53
Camp Upton, Long Island (NY), Vol. 4: 84
capitalism, Vol. 4: 28–29, 122
Caprio, Joyce E., Vol. 5: *123*
Carroll, Charles, Vol. 1: 111
Catt, Carrie Chapman, Vol. 4: 113, 117
CEA. *See* Constitutional Equality Amendment
censure, Vol. 3: 29
Center for Individual Rights (CIR), Vol. 5: 103–104, 109
Central Intelligence Agency (CIA), Vol. 5: 89, 91, 94
Central Pacific Railroad, Vol. 4: 32, 33
Central Powers. *See* Triple Alliance (the Central Powers)
chad, Vol. 5: 128
Chambers, Whittaker, Vol. 5: 26, *27*
Charles I, King of England, Vol. 1: 13
Charles II, King of England, Vol. 1: 37, 38, 39
charter, Vol. 1: 133
Chase, Salmon, Vol. 3: 79–80
Chase, Samuel, Vol. 1: 106, 109
Chauncy, Charles, Vol. 1: 67, 68
Cherokee, Vol. 3: 12–13, 14–15
Chickasaw, Vol. 3: 14
China, Vol. 5: 48, 54, 55–56, 91
Chinese Exclusion Act, Vol. 4: 32–40, *33*, *37*, *38*
Chisholm, Shirley, Vol. 5: 83
Choctaw, Vol. 3: 14
Christianity, Vol. 1: 60–68, *62*, 64
Christians, Vol. 1: 42–50
CIA. *See* Central Intelligence Agency
CIR. *See* Center for Individual Rights
civil rights
    Vol. 3: *112*, 112–120, *116*
    Vol. 5: 133
Civil Rights Act of 1866
    Vol. 3: 113–114, 119, 124
Civil Rights Act of 1875
    Vol. 4: 53–54
Civil Rights Act of 1964, Vol. 5: 100, 101, 104
Civil War, Vol. 3: 96–100, 103–104, 105
Civilian Conservation Corps, Vol. 4: 126
Clark, Kenneth, Vol. 5: 42
Clay, Henry
    Vol. 2:
        American System and, 124
        elections of 1824 and, 107–112
        Missouri Compromise and, 89, 90
        nullification and, 128–129
        political history of, 81
        portrait of, *110*
    Vol. 3:
        BUS and, 24–25
        Compromise of 1850 and, 66–67, 68, 69–70
Cleveland, Grover, Vol. 4: 60
Clinton, Bill
    Vol. 3: 126
    Vol. 5:
        Al Gore and, 122
        Fred Korematsu and, *21*
        impeachment of, 112–120, *115*, *117*
        Travelgate, 89
Clinton, Hillary Rodham, Vol. 5: 112
Coercive Acts, Vol. 1: 80
Coffee, Linda, Vol. 5: 66
Cold War
    Vol. 5:
        anti-Communism, 24–34, *27*, *28*, *30*
        Iran-Contra affair and, 88–89
        Vietnam War and, 48, 54, 55–56
Coleman, Mary Sue, Vol. 5: 105
colleges, Vol. 1: 63. *See also* universities, affirmative action in
Common Sense (Paine), Vol. 1: 97–98, 99, 101
communication
    Vol. 1: 9
    Vol. 2: 9
    Vol. 3: 9
    Vol. 4: 9
    Vol. 5: 9
communism
    Vol. 4: 28–29
    Vol. 5:
        Cold War anti-Communism, 24–34, *27*, *28*, *30*
        Iran-Contra affair and, 88–89
        Vietnam War and, 48, 49–50, 52, 54, 55–56
The Communist Manifesto (Marx and Engels), Vol. 4: 43
Compromise of 1850, Vol. 3: 62–70, 68
Concord (MA), Vol. 1: 83, 84–85
Confederacy, Vol. 3: 96–100

Confederate States of America, Vol. 3: 96–100, 102
confederation, Vol. 1: 133
Congregationalism, Vol. 1: 18, 60, 61–68
Congregationalists. *See* Puritans
Congress. *See* U.S. Congress
conservative, Vol. 5: 133
conspiracy
    Vol. 3: 133
    Vol. 4: 133
Constitution, U.S.
    Vol. 1: 124–131, *127, 132*
    Vol. 2: 86
    Vol. 3: 92, 102
    Vol. 5: 131
Constitutional Convention, Vol. 1: 107–108, 113–122, *118, 121*
Constitutional Equality Amendment (CEA), Vol. 5: 81
Constitutional Union Party, Vol. 3: 94
Continental Army, Vol. 1: 92
Continental Congress, Vol. 1: 94–98, 102, 104–106
contras, Vol. 5: 89, 91, 94
Coolidge, Calvin, Vol. 4: 122
Cooper, Thomas, Vol. 2: 103
Corey, Giles, Vol. 1: 45
"corrupt bargain," Vol. 2: 109–112
corruption
    Vol. 1: 133
    Vol. 3: 133
    Vol. 4: 133
    Vol. 5: 133
Cosby, William, Vol. 1: 52–54, 55
Cotton, John, Vol. 1: 17–18, 19, *19*
Craig, Gregory, Vol. 5: *115*
Crawford, William, Vol. 2: 106
Creek, Vol. 3: 14
Crittenden, John, Vol. 3: 95, 100
Cuba, Vol. 4: 60–68, *61, 63*
Cunningham, Milton J., Vol. 4: 57–58
Currie, Bettie, Vol. 5: 114
Czechoslovakia, Vol. 5: 26

D

Daughters of Liberty, Vol. 1: 73
Davenport, James, Vol. 1: 66, 68
Davis, Jefferson, Vol. 3: 96
Davis, John W., Vol. 5: 44–45
Dawes, William, Vol. 1: 83
Deane, Silas, Vol. 1: 104
The Death of Outrage (Bennett), Vol. 5: 119
death penalty, Vol. 1: 42
debatable issues
    Vol. 1: 7–9
    Vol. 2: 7–9
    Vol. 3: 7–9
    Vol. 4: 7–9
    Vol. 5: 7–9
Declaration of Independence
    Vol. 1:
        Abigail Adams, *100*
        arguments against independence, 99–102
        debate for independence, 95–99
        precursors to, 92–94
        writing of, 94–95, 96
"Declaration of the Causes and Necessity of Taking Up Arms" (Dickinson and Jefferson), Vol. 1: 92
"Declaration in the Name of the People" (Bacon), Vol. 1: 38
"Declaration of Rights and Sentiments" (Stanton)
    Vol. 3: 58
    Vol. 4: 110
Declaratory Act, Vol. 1: 77–78
DeJarnette, Daniel, Vol. 3: 98
Delancey, James, Vol. 1: 53, 54, 55–56
Delancey, Stephen, Vol. 1: 52
de Lôme, Enrique Dupuy, Vol. 4: 62
Democratic Party
    Vol. 3:
        civil rights for African Americans and, 117, 119
        Compromise of 1850 and, 67, 69
        emancipation and, 106
        slavery and, 93
        Texas annexation and, 36–38
        Thirteenth Amendment and, 109
    Vol. 4:
        Chinese and, 36
        election of 1876 and, 12–20
        League of Nations and, 93–94
        Prohibition and, 104
    Vol. 5: 116, 117, 122–132
Democratic-Republican Party
    Vol. 2:
        Alien and Sedition Acts and, 25–28
        defense of Embargo Acts, 69–70
        elections issues of 1800, 38–40
        Jay's Treaty and, 15–16, 17, 20
        overview of, 12
        War of 1812 and, 81–82, 84
        XYZ affair and, 23
depression, Vol. 3: 22
despotism
    Vol. 1: 133
    Vol. 3: 133
    Vol. 4: 133
Detroit Free Press, Vol. 3: 78
Dewey, George, Vol. 4: 63
DeWitt, John, Vol. 5: 19, 21
Dickens, Charles, Vol. 2: 104
Dickinson, John, Vol. 1: 92, 93, 102, 105
Diem, Ngo Dinh, Vol. 5: 49, 50, 51
discrimination
    Vol. 3: 133
    Vol. 4: 133
    Vol. 5: 133.
    See also racism; reverse discrimination
dissenting
    Vol. 3: 133
    Vol. 4: 133
    Vol. 5: 133
disunion, Vol. 3: 64
Doe v. Bolton, Vol. 5: 67
Donelson, Andrew Jackson, Vol. 2: 111
Douglass, Frederick, Vol. 3: 54, 103
Douglas, Stephen
    Vol. 3:
        in election of 1860, 93, 94, *94*
        Kansas-Nebraska Act of, 73
        Nebraska Territory and, 77
        portrait of, *79*
        secession of Southern states and, 100
Douglas, William O., Vol. 5: 34
draft, Vol. 5: 58, 59
Dred Scott case, Vol. 3: 82–90, 83
Duane, William, Vol. 3: 25
Du Bois, W.E.B., Vol. 5: 45
due process, Vol. 4: 56, 57–58
Durbin, Richard, Vol. 5: 120
Dutch Reformed Church, Vol. 1: 60, 64

E

Easton, John, Vol. 1: 29
economy (1930s), Vol. 4: 122–132
education
    Vol. 5:
        affirmative action, 100–110, *101, 103, 104, 107*
        Brown v. Board of Education, 36–46, *38, 44*
Edwards, Jonathan, Vol. 1: 62, *62*, 63, 65
Eighteenth Amendment, Vol. 4: 102–103, *106, 107*
Eisenhower, Dwight, Vol. 5: 46, 49, 56
election of 1800, Vol. 2: 32–40
election of 1824, Vol. 2: 106–112, *107*
election of 1876, Vol. 4: 12–20, *13, 16, 18*
election of 2000. *See* presidential election of 2000
Electoral College
    Vol. 2: 35
    Vol. 5: 123
Electoral Commission, Vol. 4: *16*, 16–20
electoral vote
    Vol. 4: 14–20
    Vol. 5: 123
electors, Vol. 2: 34, 35
Elliot, Roderick, Vol. 5: 38
Ellsberg, Daniel, Vol. 5: 60
El Salvador, Vol. 5: 88–89, 90

"Emancipation Proclamation" (Lincoln), Vol. 3: 104–107
embargo, Vol. 5: 133
Embargo of 1808, Vol. 2: 8, 64–72
Emerson, Irene, Vol. 3: 82–83
Enforcement Act, Vol. 2: 68, 72
Engel, George, Vol. 4: 47
England, Vol. 2: 96. *See also* Great Britain
English settlers, Vol. 1: 22–30, *24, 26*
Equal Rights Amendment (ERA), Vol. 5: *76,* 76–86, *80, 84*
Equality League of Self-Supporting Women, Vol. 4: 113
Ervin, Sam, Jr., Vol. 5: 83, 84
espionage, Vol. 5: 133
Europe, Vol. 2: 22–23
Evangelical Church Army, Vol. 4: *101*
Evans, Oliver, Vol. 4: 72
The Examiner—Defended in a Fair and Sober Answer (Williams), Vol. 1: 18
executive branch, Vol. 1: 125
Executive Order 9066, Vol. 5: 13, 19, 20–21
executive privilege, Vol. 2: 57
expansion, Vol. 3: 73–75
Ex parte Endo, Vol. 5: 17
external taxes, Vol. 1: 75

F
factions, Vol. 1: 133
farming, Vol. 2: 101, 103
FDIC. *See* Federal Deposit Insurance Corporation
Federal Bureau of Investigation (FBI), Vol. 5: 20, 25, 26–27, 31
Federal Deposit Insurance Corporation (FDIC), Vol. 4: 126
federal government, Vol. 1: 124
Federal Reserve Board, Vol. 4: 123
Federal Reserve System, Vol. 4: 123
The Federalist Papers (Madison, Hamilton, and Jay), Vol. 1: 126
Federalist Party
    Vol. 2:
        Alien and Sedition Acts and, 28–29
        criticism of Embargo Acts, 70–72
        election of 1800, 36–37
        opposition to Louisiana Purchase, 46–48
        opposition to War of 1812, 83–84
        overview of, 12
        Sedition Act and, 25
federalists, Vol. 1: 125–132
The Feminine Mystique (Friedan), Vol. 5: 77, 78
feminism, Vol. 5: 77–86
Ferdinand, Franz, Archduke of Austria, Vol. 4: 80
Ferguson, John, Vol. 4: 54, 55
Ferraro, Geraldine, Vol. 4: 120
fetus, Vol. 5: 62, 63, 67, 73–74

Field, David Dudley, Vol. 4: 18
Fielden, Samuel, Vol. 4: 44, 47
Fifteenth Amendment
    Vol. 3: 115, 116, *116,* 117–120
    Vol. 4: 53
Filene, Edward, Vol. 4: 129
filibustering, Vol. 3: 34
Finkbine, Sherri, Vol. 5: 65–66, 66
First Amendment
    Vol. 2: 26
    Vol. 4: 49
First Continental Congress, Vol. 1: 81, 87, 88–89, 92, 104
The First Great Awakening, Vol. 2: 115
First New Deal, Vol. 4: 126
Fischer, Adolph, Vol. 4: 47
Fiske, Robert, Vol. 5: 112
Florida
    Vol. 2: 45, 54
    Vol. 4: 17–18, 19, 20
    Vol. 5: 122–132
Florida Supreme Court, Vol. 5: 125, 127, 129, 131, 132
flywheel magneto, Vol. 4: 73
Folsom, Nathaniel, Vol. 1: 110
Force Bill, Vol. 2: 127–128
Ford, Gerald, Vol. 5: 108, 119–120
Ford, Henry, Vol. 4: *70,* 70–78, *71, 76,* 88
Ford Motor Company, Vol. 4: *70,* 70–78, *76*
442nd Regimental Combat Team, Vol. 5: 17
"Fourteen Points" speech, Vol. 4: 90–91
Fourteenth Amendment
    Vol. 3: 114–120
    Vol. 4: 52–53, 56, 58, 111
    Vol. 5: 42, 45, 81, 82, 101, 104, 107–108, 110
France
    Vol. 1: 101
    Vol. 2: 22–23, 36, 43–44, 64, 74–75
    Vol. 4: 91
    Vol. 5: 48–49, 50
Frankfurter, Felix, Vol. 5: 19
Franklin, Benjamin, Vol. 1: 74, 94, 96, *96,* 104–105, 108
Freedmen's Bureau, Vol. 3: 115
freedom of the press, Vol. 1: 52–58
Free-Soil Party, Vol. 3: 64
Frelinghuysen, Jacob, Vol. 1: 63
Frelinghuysen, Theodore, Vol. 3: 19, *19*
Frémont, John C., Vol. 3: *74*
French Indochina, Vol. 5: 49
French Revolution, Vol. 2: 12–13
Friedan, Betty, Vol. 5: 77, 78
Fronterio, Sharron, Vol. 5: 82
Fronterio v. Richardson, Vol. 5: 82
Fuchs, Klaus, Vol. 5: 29
fugitive
    Vol. 3: 133
    Vol. 4: 133
Fugitive Slave Law of 1850, Vol. 3: 65, 67–68

G
Gage, Thomas, Vol. 1: 80, 81, 82–83
Gaines, Lloyd, Vol. 5: 37–38
Gallatin, Albert, Vol. 2: 25–26, *27,* 68
Galloway, Joseph, Vol. 1: 88–89, 90
Garrison, William Lloyd
    Vol. 2: 117, *118*
    Vol. 3: 53
Gary, Joseph, Vol. 4: 48
Geneva Accords, Vol. 5: 50
George III, King of England, Vol. 1: 70, 80, 81, 93, 95, 97
Georgia
    Vol. 2: 128
    Vol. 3: 12–13
German Americans, Vol. 5: 14
Germany, Vol. 4: 81–85, 86, 88, 91, 125
Gerry, Elbridge, Vol. 1: 126
Gilman, Nicholas, Vol. 1: 118
Ginsburg, Ruth Bader, Vol. 5: 107–108
gold, Vol. 3: 63
Goldwater, Barry, Vol. 5: 91, 97
Gompers, Samuel, Vol. 4: 27
Gonzalez, Henry, Vol. 5: 96
Good, Sarah, Vol. 1: 43, 44–45
Gore, Al
    Vol. 4: 20
    Vol. 5: 122–132
government
    Vol. 1:
        Articles of Confederation, 104–112
        Constitutional Convention, 113–122
        Constitution, ratification of, 124–131
gradualists, Vol. 2: 122
Grand Council, Vol. 1: 88–89
Grant, Ulysses S.
    Vol. 3: 125, 127
    Vol. 4: 13
Grantham, Thomas, Vol. 1: 36, 37
Gratz, Jennifer, Vol. 5: 103–104, *104,* 105
Gratz v. Bollinger, Vol. 5: 104, 105, 107
Great Awakening, Vol. 1: 60–68, *62, 64*
Great Britain
    Vol. 1: 70–78, 80–90, 92–102
    Vol. 2: 13–14, 64–68, 74–76
    Vol. 3: 35, 48
    Vol. 4: 81–83, 85, 86, 88, 91. *See also* War of 1812
Great Compromise, Vol. 1: 122
Great Depression, Vol. 4: 108, 124–132
Great Strike of 1877, Vol. 4: 22–30, *24,* 28
Green Party, Vol. 5: 124
Greene, Nathanael, Vol. 1: 97
Grenville, George, Vol. 1: 70–71, 76

Grimes, James, Vol. 3: 132
Grimké, Sarah, Vol. 3: 57
Grinnell, Julius, Vol. 4: 47, 48, 49
Griswold v. Connecticut, Vol. 5: 71
Grutter, Barbara, Vol. 5: *104,* 104–105, 110
Grutter v. Bollinger, Vol. 5: 104–105, 110
Gulf of Tonkin, Vol. 5: 53
Gurin, Patricia, Vol. 5: 106

H

Hall, Fawn, Vol. 5: 97
Hamacher, Patrick, Vol. 5: 103–104, *104*
Hamilton, Alexander
    Vol. 1:
        Articles of Confederation and, 115
        as Federalist leader, 32
        The Federalist Papers, 126
        life of, 116
        ratification of Constitution and, 127, 130–131
    Vol. 2:
        duel with Aaron Burr, 53
        during elections of 1800, 36–37
        Federalist Party and, 12
        Jay's Treaty and, 16, 18–20
        portrait of, *19, 32,* 53
Hamilton, Andrew, Vol. 1: 54, 55, 56–58, *57*
Hancock, John, Vol. 1: 83
Harding, Warren, Vol. 4: 96, 122
Harlan, John Marshall, Vol. 4: 57
Harper's Weekly magazine
    Vol. 3: 128
    Vol. 4: 30, 40
Harris, Katherine, Vol. 5: 124–125, 126, 128
Harrison, William Henry, Vol. 2: 77, 79
Hawaii, Vol. 5: 12, 13, 14
Hawley, Joseph, Vol. 4: 39
Hayes, George E.C., Vol. 5: *38*
Hayes, Rutherford B.
    Vol. 4:
        Chinese Exclusion Act and, 35
        election of 1876 and, *13,* 13–20
        Great Strike of 1877 and, 25, 26, 29
    Vol. 5: 126
Haymarket Affair, Vol. 4: 42–50, *45, 46*
Haymarket Monument, Vol. 4: 50
"healing witches," Vol. 1: 42
Hearst, William Randolph, Vol. 4: 60
Henry, Patrick, Vol. 1: 75, 87
Herrick, Robert, Vol. 4: 87
Hirabayashi, Gordon, Vol. 5: 16–17, 18
Hiss, Alger, Vol. 5: 26, *28,* 28
Hobson, Richard, Vol. 4: 102, 106
Ho Chi Minh, Vol. 5: 48, 49

Hollywood, Vol. 5: 25
Honduras, Vol. 5: 90
Hook, Sidney, Vol. 5: 32–33
Hoover, Herbert, Vol. 4: 122, 124–125, 129, *132*
Hoover, J. Edgar, Vol. 5: 31
House Judiciary Committee, Vol. 5: 116, 118
House of Representatives. *See* U.S. House of Representatives
House Un-American Activities Committee (HUAC), Vol. 5: 25–26, 28, 31
Houston, Charles, Vol. 5: 37
Houston, Sam, Vol. 3: 32, 33, *33*
Howells, William Dean, Vol. 4: 49
HUAC. *See* House Un-American Activities Committee
Hubbard, Elizabeth, Vol. 1: 43
Hutchinson, Anne, Vol. 1: 14, *15*
Hutchinson, Thomas, Vol. 1: 73

I

Illinois, Vol. 5: 131
immigrants, Vol. 4: 112
immigration
    Vol. 4: 32–40, *33, 37, 38*
    Vol. 5: 12
impeachment
    Vol. 3: 122–132, *127, 129, 130, 131*
    Vol. 5: 96, 112–120, *115, 117*
imperialism, Vol. 4: 64–68
impressment, Vol. 2: 17, 65–66
inauguration
    Vol. 3: 133
    Vol. 4: 133
independence. *See* Declaration of Independence
Indian Removal Act, Vol. 3: 12–20
induced abortion, Vol. 5: 63
industrial policies of Henry Ford, Vol. 4: 70, 70–78, *71,* 76
industry, Vol. 2: 96–104, 124
Inglis, Charles, Vol. 1: 101
interchangeable parts, Vol. 4: 72, 73
interest rates, Vol. 4: 123
intern, Vol. 5: 133
internal tax, Vol. 1: 75
internment of Japanese Americans, Vol. 5: 12–22, *13, 15, 21*
Iran, Vol. 5: 92–93, 94
Iran-Contra affair, Vol. 5: 88–98, *90, 92, 96*
Irreconcilables, Vol. 4: 95
isolationism, Vol. 4: 95. *See also* neutrality, American
Israel, Vol. 5: 93
Issei (first generation), Vol. 5: 12
Italian Americans, Vol. 5: 14

J

Jackson, Andrew
    Vol. 2:
        elections of 1824 and, 107, 108–109
        Indian removal and, 128

        nullification and, 127, 131–132
    Vol. 3:
        BUS and, 22–27
        Indian removal and, 17–18, 20
        Indian Removal Act and, 13–14
        portrait of, *26*
        Texas annexation and, 34
Jackson, Robert, Vol. 5: 21
Jamestown (VA), Vol. 1: 34, 35, 36
Japanese Americans, internment of, Vol. 5: 12–22, *13, 15, 21*
Jay, John
    Vol. 1: 117, 126, 132, *132*
    Vol. 2: 14–15, *17,* 18
Jay's Treaty, Vol. 2: 14–20
Jefferson, Thomas
    Vol. 1:
        Aaron Burr and, 52
        Declaration of Independence and, 8, 94–95, 96, 97
        as Democratic-Republican leader, 32–33
        ratification of Constitution and, 128
        writer of "Declaration of the Causes and Necessity of Taking Up Arms," 92
    Vol. 2:
        Burr Conspiracy and, 56
        Democratic-Republican Party and, 12
        elections of 1800 and, 35–36, 38–40
        Embargo Acts and, 66–70
        expansion and, 42
        on Louisiana, 44
        Louisiana Purchase and, 45, 49–50
        portrait of, *19,* 40
    Vol. 4: 8
    Vol. 5: 8
Jeffreys, Herbert, Vol. 1: 39
Jenyns, Soame, Vol. 1: 78
Jews, Vol. 1: 60
"Jim Crow" laws
    Vol. 4: 53–54, *54,* 55
    Vol. 5: 36
Johnson, Andrew
    Vol. 3:
        civil rights and, 112–120
        impeachment of, 8, 122–132, *127, 129, 130, 131*
        Thirteenth Amendment and, 104
    Vol. 5: 116
Johnson, Hiram, Vol. 4: 95
Johnson, Lyndon B., Vol. 5: 50–53, 56, 58, 60
Jones, Paula, Vol. 5: 112–113, 114
Jordan, Vernon, Vol. 5: 113
Journal (New York newspaper), Vol. 4: 60
Joyce, Charles, Vol. 4: 39
judicial branch, Vol. 1: 125

jury nullification, Vol. 1: 57, 58

K

Kansas, Vol. 3: 73, 75–76, 77
Kansas-Nebraska Act, Vol. 3: 72–80, 74
Kearney, Dennis, Vol. 4: 38
Kendall, David, Vol. 5: *115*, 120
Kennedy, John F., Vol. 5: 49–50, 100
Kennedy, Robert F., Vol. 5: 60
Kentucky, Vol. 2: 27
Kentucky Resolutions, Vol. 2: 72, 130
Kerry, John, Vol. 5: 98
Khomeini, Ruhollah, Vol. 5: 92–93
King, Martin Luther, Jr., Vol. 5: 59
King Philip's War, Vol. 1: 22–30, *24*
King, Rufus, Vol. 2: 91, *92*, 93
Kissinger, Henry, Vol. 5: 54, 55
Klann, William, Vol. 4: 77
Knox, Henry, Vol. 2: *19*
Kohut, Andrew, Vol. 5: 117
Korean War, Vol. 5: 48, 49
Korematsu, Fred, Vol. 5: 18, *21*
Korematsu v. United States, Vol. 5: 17, 18, 19, 21, 22
Kristol, William, Vol. 5: 131

L

labor movement
    Vol. 4:
        Great Strike of 1877, 22–30
        Haymarket Affair, 42–50, *45*, 46
labor unions. *See* unions
La Follette, Robert, Vol. 4: 88
laissez-faire policies, Vol. 4: 128
land, Vol. 1: 27–30, 110–111
Laos, Vol. 5: 50, 53
Latin America, Vol. 4: 80
latitude
    Vol. 3: 133
    Vol. 4: 133
Lawson, Deodat, Vol. 1: 47
LDF. *See* Legal Defense Fund
League to Enforce Peace (LEP), Vol. 4: 98
League of Nations, Vol. 4: 8, 89–98, *92*, 97
Lebanon, Vol. 5: 93, 94
Le Duc Tho, Vol. 5: 54
Lee, Richard Henry, Vol. 1: 94, 105
Legal Defense Fund (LDF), Vol. 5: 36, 37
legislative branch, Vol. 1: 125
legislature, Vol. 1: 133
Lenin, Vladimir, Vol. 5: 24, 33
Leonard, Daniel, Vol. 1: 89
LEP. *See* League to Enforce Peace
Lewinsky, Monica, Vol. 5: 113–120
Lexington (MA), Vol. 1: 83–84, 89
liberal, Vol. 5: 133
The Liberator, Vol. 2: *117*
Lincoln, Abraham
    Vol. 3:
        freeing of the slaves and, 102–110

murder of, 122
photograph of, 97
portrait of, 105
Reconstruction and, 112
response to Dred Scott case, 90
secession of Southern states and, 93–100, *94*
    Vol. 4: 12
Lincoln's Legal Loyal League, Vol. 3: 106
Lingg, Louis, Vol. 4: 47
Livingston, Edward, Vol. 2: 26
Livingston, Robert
    Vol. 1: 94, 96, 102
    Vol. 2: 16
Lodge, Henry Cabot, Vol. 4: 65, 66, 95–96
Long, Huey, Vol. 4: 131
Louisiana, Vol. 2: 43–44
Louisiana Purchase, Vol. 2: 42–50
Louisiana Territory, Vol. 2: 42
Love, Ken, Vol. 5: 59
Lowell, Francis Cabot, Vol. 2: 97, 98, 99
Lowell (MA), Vol. 2: 99–100
Lowell System, Vol. 2: 97–99
Loyalists, Vol. 1: 90
Lum, Dyer, Vol. 4: 49
Lusitania, Vol. 4: 85, 86, 86
Lynch, Thomas, Jr., Vol. 1: 110

M

Madison, James
    Vol. 1: 117–121, *121*, 126, 128, 131
    Vol. 2: 16, 18, 69, 76, 78–81, 130, 131
Maine
    Vol. 2: 88
    Vol. 3: 62
Manhattan Project, Vol. 5: 29
Manifest Destiny
    Vol. 3: 42–43, 46–47
    Vol. 4: 64–65
Marshall, George, Vol. 5: 29
Marshall, John, Vol. 2: 37, 56–58, 59
Marshall, Thurgood, Vol. 5: 37, 38, 38–46
Martin, Luther, Vol. 2: 57
Marx, Karl
    Vol. 4: 28, 42, 43
    Vol. 5: 24, 25
Marxist Leninism, Vol. 5: 24
Maryland, Vol. 1: 106, 111
Mason, George, Vol. 1: 125
mass production, Vol. 4: 71–73, 74–75, 77, 122
Massachusetts, Vol. 1: 42–50, *46*, 48, 80–90, 116
Massasoit. *See* Usamequin (Massasoit)
Mather, Cotton, Vol. 1: 19, 30, 48, 48–49
McCarthy, Joseph, Vol. 5: 29–34, 30
McCarthyism, Vol. 5: 30–34
McCorvey, Norma, Vol. 5: 66–67, 68, 68
McDuffie, George, Vol. 2: 122
McFarlane, Robert, Vol. 5: 93, 94

McKean, Thomas, Vol. 2: 39
McKinley, William, Vol. 4: *61*, 61–62
McLaurin, George, Vol. 5: 38
McLaurin v. Oklahoma State Regents, Vol. 5: 38
McLean, John, Vol. 3: 89
Metacomet (King Philip), Vol. 1: 23–30
Methodism, Vol. 2: 115
Mexican War, Vol. 3: 42–50, *45*
Mexico
    Vol. 2: 54–55
    Vol. 3: 32–34, 42–50
    Vol. 4: 82
militia, Vol. 1: 133
minorities. *See* affirmative action; African Americans; Japanese Americans, internment of
Minutemen, Vol. 1: 81, 82, 83–84, *84*
miscarriage, Vol. 5: 63
Mississippi, Vol. 3: 102, 106, 108, 114
Mississippi River, Vol. 2: 42
Missouri, Vol. 3: 62, 75, 82, 84
Missouri Compromise
    Vol. 2: 86–94
    Vol. 3: 72, 73, 78
Model T, Vol. 4: 70, 71, 72, 75, 76
Mondale, Walter, Vol. 4: 120
Monroe Doctrine, Vol. 4: 80, 95, 98
Monroe, James
    Vol. 2: 89, 106
    Vol. 4: 80, 95
Morris, Gouverneur, Vol. 1: 58
Morris, Lewis, Vol. 1: 53–54
Mott, Lucretia
    Vol. 3: 54, 55
    Vol. 4: 110
Murphy, Frank, Vol. 5: 21, 22
Murray, Judith Sargent Stevens, Vol. 3: 52
Myrdal, Gunnar, Vol. 5: 43

N

NAACP. *See* National Association for the Advancement of Colored People
Nabrit, James M., Vol. 5: 38
Nader, Ralph, Vol. 5: 124
NARAL. *See* National Association for the Reform of Abortion Laws
Narragansett, Vol. 1: 22, 26, 29
National American Woman Suffrage Association (NAWSA), Vol. 4: 112, 113
National Association for the Advancement of Colored People (NAACP), Vol. 5: 36–38, 39
National Association for the Reform of Abortion Laws (NARAL), Vol. 5: 71
National Labor Union (NLU), Vol. 4: 23
National Organization for Women (NOW), Vol. 5: 78–81, 80

National Right to Life Committee, Vol. 5: 69
National Security Council (NSC), Vol. 5: 91, 93
National Woman Suffrage Association (NWSA), Vol. 4: 110, 112
National Woman's Party (NWP), Vol. 4: 113–114, *114*, *117*
Native Americans
    Vol. 1: 14, 16, 22–30, *24*, *26*, 32–40
    Vol. 3: 12–20
naturalization
    Vol. 3: 133
    Vol. 4: 133
Naturalization Act, Vol. 2: 24, 26
navy, Vol. 2: 78
NAWSA. *See* National American Woman Suffrage Association
Nebraska, Vol. 3: 73
Nebraska Association Opposed to Woman Suffrage, Vol. 4: 120
Neebe, Oscar, Vol. 4: 47
neutrality, American, Vol. 4: 81, 87
New Deal, Vol. 4: 122–132, *127*, 132
New England, Vol. 2: 83–84, 97–98
New Jersey, Vol. 3: 58
New Jersey Plan, Vol. 1: 120–122
"New Lights," Vol. 1: 65–68
New Mexico
    Vol. 3: 64
    Vol. 5: 122
New Orleans (LA), Vol. 2: 42, 44–45
New York
    Vol. 1: 52–58
    Vol. 5: 64
New York Gazette, Vol. 1: 53
New York Times, Vol. 4: 29
New York Weekly Journal, Vol. 1: 53–54
Newton, Isaac, Vol. 1: 61
Nicaragua, Vol. 5: 89, 90–91
1950 Internal Security Act, Vol. 5: 33
Nineteenth Amendment
    Vol. 4: 110–120, *114*, *117*
    Vol. 5: 76, 76, 77
Nisei (second generation), Vol. 5: 12, 20–21
Nixon, Richard
    Vol. 3: 126
    Vol. 5: Equal Rights Amendment and, 79
    Vietnam War and, 53–54, 55, 57, 60
    Watergate, 89, 96, 116
NLU. *See* National Labor Union
The North, Vol. 2: 90–93
North Korea, Vol. 5: 29, 48
North Vietnam, Vol. 5: 49–60
North, Lord, Vol. 1: 82
North, Oliver, Vol. 5: 91–92, *92*, 93, 94–95, 97, 98
Northwest Ordinance, Vol. 2: 87

NOW. *See* National Organization for Women
NSC. *See* National Security Council
Nullification Crisis, Vol. 2: 124–132
NWP. *See* National Woman's Party
NWSA. *See* National Woman Suffrage Association

O

obiter dictum, Vol. 3: 89
O'Connor, Sandra Day, Vol. 5: 107
"Old Ironsides," Vol. 2: 78
"Old Lights," Vol. 1: 65–68
Oliver, Andrew, Vol. 1: 72
Olson, Culbert, Vol. 5: 19
Operation Rescue, Vol. 5: 69
Oregon
    Vol. 4: 15
    Vol. 5: 122
Osborne, Sarah, Vol. 1: 43, 44–45
Otis, James, Vol. 1: 76

P

Paine, Thomas
    Vol. 1: 97–98, 99, 101
    Vol. 2: 48–49
Palm Beach County (FL), Vol. 5: *128*, 129
Panama Canal, Vol. 4: 80
Parker, John, Vol. 1: 83–84
Parliament
    Vol. 1:
        American Revolution and, 82, 90
        Coercive Acts passed by, 80
        Prohibitory Act, 94
        Stamp Act crisis and, 70, 71, 73–78
Parris, Samuel, Vol. 1: 43, 44, 47
Parsons, Albert, Vol. 4: 44, 47, 50
Parsons, Lucy, Vol. 4: 50
Paterson, William, Vol. 1: 120
Patriots, Vol. 1: 80–90
Paul, Alice
    Vol. 4: 113, 115, *117*
    Vol. 5: 76, 76
Pearl Harbor (HI), Vol. 5: 13
Pennsylvania Railroad, Vol. 4: 25, 26
"Pentagon Papers," Vol. 5: 60
perjury, Vol. 5: 115, 117
Perot, Ross, Vol. 5: 112
Pershing, John "Black Jack," Vol. 4: 82–83, *83*
petition
    Vol. 1: 133
    Vol. 3: 133
    Vol. 4: 133
Philadelphia (PA), Vol. 1: 92
Philippines, Vol. 4: 63, 64, 65, 66, 67–68
Phips, Mary, Vol. 1: 46
Phips, William, Vol. 1: 45, 46–47
Pickering, Timothy, Vol. 2: *71*, 71
Pierce, Franklin, Vol. 3: 73
pietism, Vol. 1: 61, 63, 68, 133

Pilgrims
    Vol. 1:
        King Philip's War and, 22–30, *24*, *26*
        Roger Williams and, 12–13, 17
Pitt, William, Vol. 1: 90
Pittsburgh (PA) strike, Vol. 4: 25
plantation
    Vol. 1: 133
    Vol. 3: 133
    Vol. 4: 133
Plessy, Homer, Vol. 4: 54–58
Plessy v. Ferguson
    Vol. 4: 52, 52–58, *54*
    Vol. 5: 36, 40, 44, 67
Plymouth (MA), Vol. 1: 13
Poindexter, John, Vol. 5: 94–95, 97
political parties, Vol. 2: 12
politics
    Vol. 2: 74–75, 91
    Vol. 3: 28, 59–60
Polk, James K.
    Vol. 3:
        Mexican War and, 46–47
        Mexico and, 42–43, *49*
        Texas annexation and, 35
        Whig Party and, 48
polls
    Vol. 3: 133
    Vol. 4: 133
Poor Richard's Almanac (Franklin), Vol. 1: 74
popular vote
    Vol. 4: 14–15
    Vol. 5: 123
Powell, Lewis, Vol. 5: 102, 105, 106
Praying Indians, Vol. 1: 25
pregnancy. *See* abortion
prejudice, Vol. 4: 34–40. *See also* racism
preparedness program, Vol. 4: 81, 82, 84–85, 87–88, 102
Presbyterians, Vol. 1: 60
Prescott, Samuel, Vol. 1: 83
presidential election of 2000, Vol. 5: 122–132, *123*, *128*, *130*
press, freedom of, Vol. 1: 52–58
privacy, right to, Vol. 5: 71, 74
Proctor, John, Vol. 1: 45
progressives, Vol. 4: 87–88
Prohibition, Vol. 4: 100–108, *101*, *106*
Prohibition Party, Vol. 4: 101
Prohibitory Act, Vol. 1: 94
propaganda, Vol. 5: 133
Protestantism, Vol. 1: 60, 61–68
Providence (RI), Vol. 1: 14
public schools. *See* schools
Pulitzer, Joseph, Vol. 4: 60
Puritans
    Vol. 1:
        Native Americans and, 27, 29–30
        Pilgrims and, 23
        Roger Williams and, 12–20, *15*, *19*
        Salem witch trials, 42–50, *46*, *48*
Putnam, Ann, Vol. 1: 43, 45, 47
Pym, William, Vol. 1: 77

Q

Quakers
- Vol. 2: 115
- Vol. 3: 52
- Vol. 4: 115

quickening, Vol. 5: 62, 63
quotas, Vol. 5: 101–102, 104

R

race. *See* affirmative action; African Americans; *Brown v. Board of Education*

racism
- Vol. 4: 39, 65, 67, 112
- Vol. 5: 12

Radical Republicans
- Vol. 3: 112–113, 115–118, 119, 123–132
- Vol. 4: 13

railroads, Vol. 4: 32, 33, 33
railroad strike of 1877, Vol. 4: 22–30, 24, 28
railroad unions, Vol. 4: 23–25
Randolph, Edmund, Vol. 2: 19
Ray, Robert, Vol. 5: 118
Reagan, Ronald, Vol. 5: 18, 88–98, 96
recession, Vol. 3: 22

Reconstruction
- Vol. 3: 112–113, 118–120, 122–132
- Vol. 4: 12, 13–14, 17, 52, 52–53

Reconstruction Finance Corporation (RFC), Vol. 4: 124–125
recounts (2000 national election), Vol. 5: 124–132, 128
Red Scare, Vol. 5: 25
Regents of the University of California v. Bakke, Vol. 5: 101, 101–102
Rehnquist, William, Vol. 5: 109

religion
- Vol. 1: 12–20, 42–50, 60–68, 62, 64
- Vol. 2: 115, 118–121
- Vol. 3: 49, 57, 59–60

Republican Party
- Vol. 3:
  - birth of, 74
  - civil rights and, 112–113, 116–120
  - in election of 1860, 93–94
  - emancipation and, 106–107
  - impeachment of Andrew Johnson and, 122–132
  - Thirteenth Amendment and, 109
- Vol. 4: 12–20, 36, 93–94
- Vol. 5: 112, 113, 116, 117, 122–132

Reservationists, Vol. 4: 93, 94, 95
Revere, Paul, Vol. 1: 83, 89
reverse discrimination, Vol. 5: 102, 104–105
revival, Vol. 1: 63–65, 133
RFC. *See* Reconstruction Finance Corporation

Rhode Island,
- Vol. 1: 14, 15, 17, 117

Rhode Island's Electoral College, Vol. 5: 123
right to privacy, Vol. 5: 71, 74
Robertson, Pat, Vol. 5: 97
Rockingham, Lord, Vol. 1: 73
Roe v. Wade,
- Vol. 5: 66–74, 68, 70

Roman Catholic Church, Vol. 5: 69, 73–74
Roosevelt, Eleanor, Vol. 5: 22
Roosevelt, Franklin
- Vol. 4: 81, 104, 125–132
- Vol. 5: 13–14, 17, 19, 20–21, 22, 28

Roosevelt, Theodore,
- Vol. 4: 63, 63

Ross, John, Vol. 3: 14–15, 20
Rough Riders, Vol. 4: 63, 63
Ruff, Charles, Vol. 5: 115, 119–120
Rutledge, James, Vol. 1: 102

S

sabotage, Vol. 5: 133
Saints, Vol. 1: 23
Salem (MA), Vol. 1: 13
Salem witch trials, Vol. 1: 42–50, 46, 48
saloons, Vol. 4: 105, 107
Sandinistas, Vol. 5: 89, 90, 94
San Francisco (CA), Vol. 4: 32–33, 34
San Francisco Chronicle, Vol. 5: 20
Santa Anna, Antonio López de, Vol. 3: 32, 33
Santiago (Cuba), Vol. 4: 63
Sassamon, Vol. 1: 25
Saudi Arabia, Vol. 5: 91
Scalia, Antonin, Vol. 5: 109
Schlafly, Phyllis, Vol. 5: 84, 84–86
Schmitz, John G., Vol. 5: 86

schools
- Vol. 5:
  - affirmative action in public universities, 100–110, 101, 103, 104, 107
  - *Brown v. Board of Education*, 36–46, 38, 44

Schroeder, Patricia, Vol. 5: 82
Schurz, Carl, Vol. 4: 66–67, 68
Schwab, Michael, Vol. 4: 47
science, Vol. 1: 61
Scott, Dred, Vol. 3: 82–90, 83
Scott, Melinda, Vol. 4: 116
Scott, Thomas, Vol. 4: 26, 29
SDS. *See* Students for a Democratic Society
secession of Southern states, Vol. 3: 92, 92–100, 94, 97
Second Continental Congress, Vol. 1: 92–93, 104
The Second Great Awakening
- Vol. 2: 115–116
- Vol. 3: 52–53

Second New Deal, Vol. 4: 126
second women's movement, Vol. 5: 77–78

SEC. *See* Security and Exchange Commission
sectionalism, Vol. 2: 91
Security and Exchange Commission (SEC), Vol. 4: 126
Sedition Act, Vol. 2: 25. *See also* Alien and Sedition Acts
seditious libel, Vol. 1: 52, 54–58

segregation
- Vol. 4: 52, 52–58, 54
- Vol. 5: 36–46, 38, 44, 100

Seminole, Vol. 3: 15
Senate. *See* U.S. Senate
Seneca Falls Convention, Vol. 3: 52–60, 55, 56
Sensenbrenner, James, Vol. 5: 118
separation of church and state, Vol. 1: 12–20, 15, 19
Separatists, Vol. 1: 12–13, 17, 23
Serbia, Vol. 4: 80
Seward, William, Vol. 3: 122
sexual rights, Vol. 5: 77
Shays, Daniel, Vol. 1: 116
Sheean, Vincent, Vol. 4: 124
Sherman, John, Vol. 4: 20
Sherman, Roger,
- Vol. 1: 94, 96, 119, 122

Shouse, Jarrett, Vol. 4: 130
Sickles, Daniel, Vol. 4: 15
Sims, Thomas, Vol. 3: 65
Six Companies, Vol. 4: 32, 35
skirmishes, Vol. 1: 133
Slater, Samuel, Vol. 2: 96

slavery
- Vol. 1:
  - Declaration of Independence and, 95
  - taxation and, 109–110
- Vol. 2:
  - depiction of slave market, 120
  - Missouri Compromise and, 86–94
  - slave owners and abolitionism, 121–122
  - slave trade, 86
  - tariffs and, 130
- Vol. 3:
  - in California/New Mexico, 62
  - freeing of the slaves, 102–110, 105, 108
  - Mexican War and, 47
  - secession of Southern states and, 92, 92–100, 94, 97
  - in Texas, 35
  - Texas annexation and, 37–38, 39. *See also* abolitionists

Smith Act of 1940, Vol. 5: 32
Smith, William, Vol. 1: 101
Smoot-Hawley Tariff, Vol. 4: 125

smuggling
- Vol. 1: 70–71
- Vol. 2: 68

socialism
- Vol. 4: 42–43, 87, 120, 128
- Vol. 5: 31

Social Security, Vol. 4: 126
Society of Friends. *See* Quakers

The South, Vol. 2: 93–94
South Carolina
    Vol. 2: 127, 130
    Vol. 3: 95, 97–98
South Carolina Exposition and Protest of 1828, Vol. 2: 131
South Korea, Vol. 5: 29, 48
South Vietnam, Vol. 5: 49–60
Southern states
    Vol. 3:
        civil rights for African Americans and, 113, 114, 115–116, 117–120
        freeing of the slaves and, 102–110
        secession of, 92, 92–100, 94, 97
sovereignty
    Vol. 1: 133
    Vol. 3: 77
Soviet Union
    Vol. 5:
        Cold War anti-Communism and, 24–34
        Iran-Contra affair and, 88–89
        Vietnam War and, 48, 54, 55–56
Spain
    Vol. 2: 43–44, 54
    Vol. 3: 32
Spanish-American War, Vol. 4: 60–68, 61, 63
Spies, August, Vol. 4: 44, 47
spontaneous abortion, Vol. 5: 63
Stalin, Joseph, Vol. 5: 24
Stamp Act Congress, Vol. 1: 73, 76
Stamp Act Crisis,
    Vol. 1: 70–78, 72, 77
Stanton, Edwin,
    Vol. 3: 125, 127, 127, 128
    Vol. 5: 116
Stanton, Elizabeth Cady
    Vol. 3: 54–55, 56, 57, 58, 119
    Vol. 4: 110
Starr, Kenneth, Vol. 5: 112–113, 114, 115, 118
steam engine, Vol. 2: 96
Stevens, John Paul, Vol. 5: 130
Stevens, Thaddeus, Vol. 3: 112, 112–113, 117, 118, 120
stock market, Vol. 4: 126
stock market crash, Vol. 4: 123–124
stocks, Vol. 4: 122
Stoddard, Solomon, Vol. 1: 62
STOP ERA, Vol. 5: 84–85, 86
Stowe, Harriet Beecher, Vol. 2: 121
Strader v. Graham, Vol. 3: 86
Strangers, Vol. 1: 23
Strike of 1877,
    Vol. 4: 22–30, 24, 28
strikes, textile mill, Vol. 2: 99
Strong, Josiah, Vol. 4: 65
Students for a Democratic Society (SDS), Vol. 5: 58
submarines, Vol. 4: 81
Suffolk Resolves, Vol. 1: 89

suffrage
    Vol. 3: 115–120, 116
    Vol. 4: 110–120, 114, 117. *See also* Seneca Falls Convention
Sugar Act, Vol. 1: 70–71
Sumner, Charles,
    Vol. 3: 50, 129, 129
Sumner, William, Vol. 3: 108–109, 112
Supreme Court. *See* U.S. Supreme Court
Susquehannock natives, Vol. 1: 32, 33, 38
Sweatt v. Painter, Vol. 5: 38
Sweitzer, Donal R., Vol. 5: 123

T
Taft, William Howard, Vol. 4: 85, 98, 102
Talmadge, Herman, Vol. 5: 46
Taney, Roger Brooke, Vol. 3: 86–87
tariffs
    Vol. 2: 124–128, 126
    Vol. 4: 125
taxation, Vol. 1: 32–40, 70–78, 109–110
Taylor, Stuart, Jr., Vol. 5: 132
Taylor, Zachary, Vol. 3: 43, 44, 45
Tecumseh, Vol. 2: 76, 77
Tell, David, Vol. 5: 131
temperance movement
    Vol. 3: 52
    Vol. 4: 100–101
Tennant, Gilbert, Vol. 1: 63, 65, 67
Tennant, William, Vol. 1: 63, 65
Tenure of Office Act, Vol. 3: 124, 125–127, 128, 130–132
territories, Vol. 3: 62–64
Tet Offensive, Vol. 5: 52
Texas
    Vol. 3: 32–40
    Vol. 5: 66–67
textile mills, Vol. 2: 97–104
therapeutic abortion exceptions, Vol. 5: 64, 65–66, 69
Thirteenth Amendment
    Vol. 3: 104, 108, 108–110, 112
    Vol. 4: 52, 56, 57, 58
Thomas, Clarence, Vol. 5: 110
Thomas, Lorenzo, Vol. 3: 125
Tilden, Samuel
    Vol. 4: 14–15, 17–20
    Vol. 5: 126
Tisquantum, Vol. 1: 22
Tituba, Vol. 1: 43, 44, 45
tobacco, Vol. 1: 32
Toombs, Robert, Vol. 3: 64
Topeka (KS), Vol. 5: 39
totalitarian government, Vol. 5: 55–56
Tourgée, Albion, Vol. 4: 54, 56
Trail of Tears, Vol. 3: 15
treason
    Vol. 1: 133
    Vol. 2: 56, 57–58

treaties
    Vol. 2: 79–80
    Vol. 3: 17–18, 45–46
Treaty of Guadeloupe-Hidalgo, Vol. 3: 45–46
Treaty of Paris, Vol. 1: 115
Treaty of Versailles, Vol. 4: 91, 92, 94, 97
Triple Alliance (the Central Powers), Vol. 4: 80, 81, 90
Triple Entente (Allies), Vol. 4: 80, 83, 84–85, 90, 91
Tripp, Linda, Vol. 5: 113, 114
Truman, Harry
    Vol. 5:
        Cold War anti-communism and, 24, 25, 29, 33–34
        segregation and, 39
        Vietnam and, 48–49
Truth, Sojourner, Vol. 3: 57
Tule Lake internment camp (CA), Vol. 5: 16
"Twelve Reasons Why Women Should Vote" (National Woman Suffrage Publishing Company), Vol. 4: 118
Twenty-first Amendment, Vol. 4: 104
Tyler, John
    Vol. 2: 128
    Vol. 3: 34–36
tyranny
    Vol. 1: 133
    Vol. 3: 133
    Vol. 4: 133

U
UCD. *See* University of California at Davis
UN. *See* United Nations
Uncle Tom's Cabin (Stowe), Vol. 2: 121
Underwood, Oscar, Vol. 4: 107
unions
    Vol. 2: 99
    Vol. 4: 23–25, 28, 30, 42–50, 45, 46, 108
    Vol. 5: 25
United Nations (UN)
    Vol. 4: 94
    Vol. 5: 29
universities, affirmative action in, Vol. 5: 100–110, 101, 103, 104, 107
University of California at Davis (UCD), Vol. 5: 100–102, 103
University of Michigan, Vol. 5: 103–110, 104, 107
Usamequin (Massasoit), Vol. 1: 22–23, 24, 27
U.S. Army
    Vol. 2: 78
    Vol. 5: 31
U.S. battleship *Maine*, Vol. 4: 61, 62
U.S. Commission on Civil Rights, Vol. 5: 129

144 Cumulative Index

U.S. Congress
  Vol. 1: 107–111, 114, 115–116
  Vol. 2: 81, 83, 86–89
  Vol. 3: 18–20, 40, 103, 104, 108–110, 113–116, 125–126, 128, 130–131
  Vol. 4: *16*, 16–20
  Vol. 5: 26, 46, 76, 77, 78–79, 81, 83–84, 88, 90, 90–91, 95–96, 115–117
U.S. House of Representatives
  Vol. 1: 124
  Vol. 2: 35–36
  Vol. 3: *108*, 109, 125, 128
  Vol. 5: 115–117
U.S. Senate
  Vol. 3: 125–126, 128, 131–132
  Vol. 4: 93–94, 96
  Vol. 5: 116, 117, 118, 120
U.S. Supreme Court
  Vol. 1: 53
  Vol. 2: 58
  Vol. 3: 86, 88–89
  Vol. 4:
    on Civil Rights Act of 1875, 53
    Plessy v. Ferguson, 54, 55–58
  Vol. 5:
    affirmative action and, *101*, 101–102, 103–106, 108–110
    Brown v. Board of Education, 39–46
    Cold War anti-communism and, 32, 34
    election of 2000 and, 125, 127, 129, *130*, 130, 131
    Equal Rights Amendment and, 81–82
    Korematsu v. United States, 17, 19, 21
    Paula Jones's case and, 114
    Roe v. Wade, 67, 69, 71, 72
    segregation and, 36, 37–38
    Utah, Vol. 4: 111
USS *Chesapeake*, Vol. 2: 65–66, 67
USS *Constitution*, Vol. 2: 78
USS *Maddox*, Vol. 5: 53

V

Valley Spirit (newspaper), Vol. 3: 107, 110
Van Buren, Martin, Vol. 3: 17, 34
Van Dam, Rip, Vol. 1: 52–53
Venona Project, Vol. 5: 26–27, 28
veto, Vol. 3: 28–29
Viet Cong, Vol. 5: 49–50, 51, 53
Vietnam War, Vol. 5: 48–60, *51*, *52*, 59
Vietnamization, Vol. 5: 53–54, 57

Villa, Pancho, Vol. 4: 82, 83
Villard, Oswald Garrison, Vol. 4: 88
Vinson, Fred, Vol. 5: 32
Virginia
  Vol. 1: 32–40, 106
  Vol. 2: 27
Virginia Plan, Vol. 1: 119–120
Volstead Act, Vol. 4: 103, 104
vote
  Vol. 1: 108–109
  Vol. 3: 115–120, *116*
  Vol. 4: 105, 110–120, *114*, *117*
  Vol. 5: 76, *76*, *77*, 122–132

W

Wade, Henry, Vol. 5: 66
wages, Vol. 4: 73–74, 75, 76, 77–78
Walker, David, Vol. 2: 116
Walker, Robert, Vol. 3: 37–38
Wall Street Journal, Vol. 4: 78
Wallace, Lew, Vol. 4: 19
Walsh, Lawrence, Vol. 5: 94–95, 96
Wampanoag, Vol. 1: 22–30
Wamsutta, Vol. 1: 23
War Hawks, Vol. 2: 81–82
War of 1812
  Vol. 2: 74–84
  Vol. 3: 92
Waring, J. Waties, Vol. 5: 39
Warren, Earl, Vol. 5: 40–41, 43
Warren, Joseph, Vol. 1: 83
Washington, George
  Vol. 1: 92, 98, 117, *118*
  Vol. 2: 19
  Vol. 4: 100
Washington, John, Vol. 1: 32
Washington Post, Vol. 5: 124
Watergate
  Vol. 3: 126
  Vol. 5: 89, 96, 116
Watson-Wentworth, Charles, Vol. 1: 73
WCTU. *See* Women's Christian Temperance Union
Webb-Kenyon Act, Vol. 4: 101–102
Webster, Daniel, Vol. 3: 28, 29, 30, 38–39, *39*
Weddington, Sarah, Vol. 5: 66, 72
Weinberger, Caspar, Vol. 5: 95
Weiner, Mark S., Vol. 5: *123*
Weiner, Susan, Vol. 5: *123*
Weld, Angelina Grimké, Vol. 3: 53
Weld, Theodore, Vol. 2: 121
Wesley, John, Vol. 2: 115
western lands, Vol. 1: 110–111
Wheeler, Wayne, Vol. 4: 103
Wheeler, William A., Vol. 4: *13*
Whig Party, Vol. 3: 35, 38–40, 47–50, 67–69
"Whiskey Rebellion," Vol. 4: 100
White, Byron, Vol. 5: 72
White, Dexter, Vol. 5: 28
White, Mark, Vol. 5: *128*
White, Samuel, Vol. 2: 48
Whitefield, George, Vol. 1: 63–65, *64*
Whitewater investigation, Vol. 5: 112–113

Whitman, Walt, Vol. 4: 22
Wilhelm II, Kaiser of Germany, Vol. 4: 84
Wilkinson, James, Vol. 2: 54–55
Williams, Roger, Vol. 1: 12–20, 29
Williams, William, Vol. 1: 106
Wilmot, David, Vol. 3: 69
Wilmot Proviso, Vol. 3: 69–70
Wilson, James, Vol. 1: 122
Wilson, Woodrow
  Vol. 4:
    League of Nations and, 90–94, 96, 97, 97–98
    suffragist movement and, 113, 115, 117
    World War I and, 81, 82, 84–85, 88, 92
Wirt, William, Vol. 2: 60
witch trials, Salem, Vol. 1: 42–50, *46*, *48*
Witherspoon, John, Vol. 1: 109
women
  Vol. 2: 99–100, *102*
  Vol. 4: 110–120, *114*, *117*
  Vol. 5: 76, 76–86, 80, *84*.
    See also Seneca Falls Convention
Women's Christian Temperance Union (WCTU), Vol. 4: 101, 112
Women's Political Union (WPU), Vol. 4: 113
Wonders of the Invisible World (Mather), Vol. 1: 49
workers, Vol. 4: 73–75, 77–78, 123
workers rights, Vol. 2: 99–100
Workingman's Party, Vol. 4: 35, 37, *37*, 38
Works Progress Administration (WPA), Vol. 4: 126, *127*
World Anti-Slavery Convention, Vol. 3: 53–54
World (newspaper), Vol. 4: 60
World War I, Vol. 4: 80–88, *83*, *84*, *86*, 102–103, 115, 117, 125
World War II, Vol. 5: *13*, 13–22, *15*, *21*, *24*
WPA. *See* Works Progress Administration
WPU. *See* Women's Political Union
Wyoming
  Vol. 3: 59
  Vol. 4: 111

X

XYZ affair, Vol. 2: 23, *24*

Y

Yalta Conference, Vol. 5: 28
Yates, Robert, Vol. 1: 130
yellow journalism, Vol. 4: 60

Z

Zenger, John Peter, Vol. 1: 53–58
Zenger trial, Vol. 1: 52–58, *54*, *57*
Zimmerman, Arthur, Vol. 4: 82

Wake Tech. Libraries
9101 Fayetteville Road
Raleigh, North Carolina 27603-5696

WAKE TECHNICAL COMMUNITY COLLEGE
3 3063 00128234 1

DATE DUE

MAY 1 6 2007			
JUN 2 6 2007			
DEC 1 0 2007			
DEC 1 6 2008			
MAR 1 6 2010			
FEB 2 8 2012			
			FEB '07

WITHDRAWN